RAMBLE
TEXAS

A Wanderer's Guide to the Offbeat, Overlooked, and Outrageous

BY

ERIC PETERSON

speck press

golden

Published by Speck Press
An imprint of Fulcrum Books
4690 Table Mountain Drive, Suite 100 • Golden, Colorado 80403
303-277-1623 • 800-992-2908 • speckpress.com

This publication is provided for informational and educational purposes. The information herein contained is true and complete to the best of our knowledge.

Library of Congress Cataloging-in-Publication Data

Peterson, Eric, 1973-
  Ramble Texas : a wanderer's guide to the offbeat, overlooked, and outrageous / by Eric Peterson.
     p. cm.
  Includes index.
  ISBN 978-1-933108-28-5 (pbk.)
  1. Texas--Tours. 2. Curiosities and wonders--Texas--Guidebooks. 3. Peterson, Eric, 1973---Travel--Texas. 4. Texas--Description and travel. I. Title.
  F384.3.P47 2010
  917.6404'64--dc22

                        2009030424

Printed in China by Golden Cup Printing Co., Ltd.

10 9 8 7 6 5 4 3 2 1

Book layout and design by Margaret McCullough

Pages 10–11, Texas map provided by Marge Mueller, © Gray Mouse Graphics

Pages 19, 32, 69, 100, 238, 239, cover, back cover © Shutterstock; pages 4, 9, 13, 55, 101, 123, 177, 221, back cover © Larry D. Moore; pages 6, 12 © Austin Convention & Visitors Bureau; pages 7, 26, 27, 30, 31, 34, 66, 75, 77, 83, 108, 118, 141, 158, 161, 172, 175, 178, 188, 190, 198, 203, 208, 217, 219, 220, 222, 224, 228, 236, 240, inset cover, back flap © Texas Tourism; page 24 © Museum of the Weird; page 25 © Museum of Natural & Artificial Ephemerata, Scott Webel; pages 54, 76, 114 © Corpus Christi Convention & Visitors Bureau; page 28 © San Jose Hotel, Allison V. Smith; pages 122, 126 (Dallas Zoo), 131 © Dallas Convention & Visitors Bureau; page 150 © Sixth Floor Museum; all other photographs © Eric Peterson. For specific information about individual photographs, please contact the publisher.

To Pampa. From your favorite grandson, Eric.

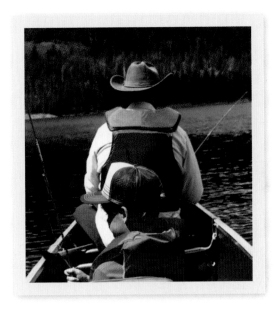

THANKS TO:

Thanks to Jay J. Johnson-Castro Sr., Sarah Boone, Eric Miller,
Abie Cox, Thomas Fawcett, Starla Simmons, Willis, Veleisa Patton,
Ashley White, Kelly Campbell, Troy, Evy, and Michelle, Lindsey Brown,
Stephen Bridges, Stuart Rosenberg, Daryl Whitworth, Katie Merrill,
Cynta de Narvaez, Nina Eastman, Derek Lawrence, Susan Hill Newton,
Margaret McCullough, Mom and Dad, everyone at the Gardner Hotel,
Michelle Horine, Pifas Silva, Veronica Castro, Larry and Babs,
Eva Aivaliotis, Bobby and Kendra Mandarich, John Neck,
Maria Elena Lucas, Diana Joe, Fabio and Virginia, and Gary Oliver.

CONTENTS

INTRODUCTION

I was standing in line at a restaurant in the Texas Hill Country when a woman asked me where I was from. "Denver," I said. She asked me what I was doing in the Lone Star State. I told her I was writing a travel book about Texas.

She scowled. "Shouldn't a Texan be writing a travel book about Texas?"

I had nothing. I mumbled something and started to cry on the inside.

Later that night at a bar, a second woman questioned my credentials as a Colorado native writing about Texas. I reassured her that my talents as a wordsmith outweighed my non-Texanness, but we both seemed to doubt my words at that particular moment in time.

Months later, the right, snappy answer finally burst into my head: every Texan has a personal vision of the true Texas. The problem is, every Texan has a *different* personal vision of the true Texas. An outsider is free to see the many sides to the story of Texas. Yep. And my dad was born in Galveston. Uh-huh. That's right, lady. Move along.

One point all Texans seem to agree on is that Texas is its own distinct place and not part of any other geographic region. Ask a Texan if the state is part of the South, or the Southwest, or any other region and you'll likely get a feisty, expletive-laden response. Especially if that Texan has been sitting next to you at a bar for several hours running.

"This ain't the [fill-in-the-mother-blanking] Southwest!" they'll probably rail. "This is [fill-in-the-blanking] Texas!"

And, to their credit, the statement is absolutely true. With the possible exception of Utah, Texas has got to be the state most likely to secede from the union into independent nationhood. Seven, not six, flags have flown over Texas—those of Spain, France, Spain again, Mexico, the Republic of Texas, the little-known Republic of the Rio Grande, the United States of America, the Confederate States of America, and the United States of America again. Why not the Republic of Texas again? (One good reason: secession has been illegal since the Civil War.)

Texas would probably do okay back on its own. This is Texas, damn't, big enough and tough enough to take on any

state or region if it came right down to it. And if Texas bordered Massachusetts or Vermont, it just might; but it borders Oklahoma and Arkansas, so things run pretty smoothly. I only hope we can avert a clash between California and Texas in a worst-postapocalyptic-case scenario.

And outside of Oklahoma and Arkansas, who view their neighbor as getting a bit too liberal for her own good, Texas is misunderstood. There are people who associate it with ex-President Dubya, and his ranch in Crawford and boyhood home in Midland, and for that reason alone do not want to ever visit the place.

Keeping in mind Bush's Connecticut birthplace, his blue-blooded pedigree, and his Ivy League education, it's time to reset your political and cultural preconceptions about Texas and dive in.

This great state is so wildly diverse, there is no categorizing it. Because of a clause in the state constitution, Texas is legally allowed to split into five separate states. Each would be distinct. The landscape varies from West Texas, bleak and depopulated, to Hill Country, with its rolling greenery and whiffs of progressivism, to the East Texas of Dallas, a city that seems to aspire to be Paris (France, that is), if only Paris weren't so damned French.

And as they say, everything is bigger in Texas. Forty-one of Texas's 254 counties are larger than Rhode Island. The Texas State Capitol, in Austin, is bigger than that of any other state. The Dallas-Fort Worth airport is bigger than Manhattan and has the world's largest parking lot. Stretching across 900 miles of Texas, US Highway 83 is the longest highway in any one state. And Houston has earned the title of the nation's fattest city several times. (However, in 2008 it was merely the tenth chubbiest. Dang.)

A gelatinous layer of faith also persists around Texas's generous midsection. And there is plenty of religious extremism, to be sure, not to mention plenty of sun-scorched wasteland with oil underneath. Actually, when you put it in those terms, Texas sounds a lot like the Middle East of the United States. Only, don't let a Texan hear you say that.

At its historic core, the state formerly known as Tejas still sits squarely at the intersection of Anglo America and Latin America on the banks of the Rio Grande. Texas only got its *x* because gringos had trouble with the *j* in the Spanish *Tejas*. The Spanish got the name from the Tejas Indians—*Tejas*, meaning "friends"—who were living in the Rio Grande Valley when the first Spanish explorers arrived.

Cowboy hats and barbecue are widely perceived as Texan innovations. Not true. We have Mexico to thank for those. Basically, without its Latin spice, Texas is a bigger, less-symmetrical Kansas, only with much of the fruitful plain replaced by desert or swamp. Yet with its proud Mexican ties, Texas transcends any other state with its remarkable southern border, also known as the Rio Bravo and the Rio Grande.

All of this far-flung history and diversity can make for a bit of a volatile combo, but it's nothing that can't be pacified with a rack of ribs and a cold six-pack, maybe some tacos. Even Texans have their soft spots.

—Eric Peterson

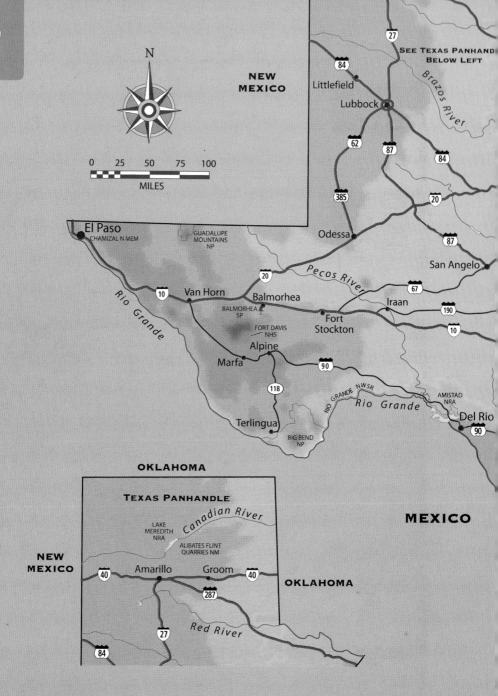

N

NEW
MEXICO

0   25   50   75   100

MILES

27

SEE TEXAS PANHANDLE
BELOW LEFT

84

Littlefield

Lubbock

Brazos River

62   87

84

385

20

El Paso
CHAMIZAL N MEM

GUADALUPE
MOUNTAINS
NP

Odessa

87

San Angelo

20

10   Van Horn   Balmorhea

Pecos River

67

BALMORHEA
SP

Iraan

190

FORT DAVIS
NHS

Fort
Stockton

10

Alpine

Rio Grande

Marfa

90

118

RIO GRANDE N W S R

AMISTAD
NRA

Terlingua

Rio Grande

Rio Grande

Del Rio

90

BIG BEND
NP

OKLAHOMA

TEXAS PANHANDLE

Canadian River

LAKE
MEREDITH
NRA

ALIBATES FLINT
QUARRIES NM

MEXICO

NEW
MEXICO

40   Amarillo   Groom   40

OKLAHOMA

287

27

Red River

84

OKLAHOMA

ARKANSAS

Red River

TEXAS

87
44
82
82
Paris
82
271
30
59

35
75

287
Plano
30
59

Fort
Worth
Weatherford
80
Grand Saline
20
Pittsburg

Dallas
45
20
259
59

LOUISIANA

bilene
20

377
Corsicana
96

Dublin
Hico
377
281

Waco
35

Trinity River

Colorado River
67

Brazos River

Sabine River

Temple
190
190
45
Huntsville
Neches River

190

LYNDON B
JOHNSON NHP
Caldwell
BIG
THICKET
N PRES

Fredricksburg
Austin
36
Brenham
59
Beaumont
10

Luckenbach
290
San
Marcos
290
Fayetteville
90

Hunt
35
Lockhart
Schulenburg
Katy
10

Bandera
173
Luling
San Jacinto River

New
Braunfels
Houston

San Antonio
10
Seguin
90a
Shiner
Colorado River
45

SAN ANTONIO
MISSIONS NHP
183
Wharton
Galveston

90
Cuero
59

Uvalde
Poteet
37
San Antonio River

Dilley
Guadalupe River

Nueces River
83
35

Freer
77

59

Laredo
Port Aransas

281
Corpus Christi
Gulf of Mexico

83
77
PADRE
ISLAND
NS

Falcon
Heights
PALO ALTO
BATTLEFIELD
NHS

Los
Ebanos
83
Hidalgo
Brownsville

AUSTIN AND HILL COUNTRY

Capitol OF TEXAS

INTRODUCTION

Many see Hill Country as Texas at its most defiantly Texan—that is to say, independent, renegade, and, of course, weird.

The political and intellectual nerve center of the state has become increasingly monetized in recent years, with new, old-looking lofts and new, new-looking towers. But Austin is still as oddball as Texas gets, with funky neighborhoods tucked into urban forests, and scads of coffee shops filled with students, slackers, and a smattering of suits and homeless people. Then there is the superlative nightlife, which includes numerous world-class music venues and just as many world-class lowlife dives.

Austin is also the home of the University of Texas, the state's biggest institution of higher learning, and the Texas State Capitol, the largest such structure in the United States. Sixth Street's legendary nightlife attracts a confluence of boozing UT students, boozing state politicians, boozing big shots, and just plain old boozing boozers. The seemingly endless strip of bars offers them all the booze they could possibly drink.

Tucked around Austin in the rolling green shag of forest are quaint tourist towns, funky old roadhouses, and the funk of roadkill. First settled largely by German and Czech immigrants in the middle 1800s, the Hill Country as a result has a heavy concentration of beer gardens—a good thing. There are plenty of crystalline rivers for tubing expeditions, on which beer is encouraged, also a good thing. Another good thing: the out-of-the-way spots where pickers get together and jam for people who drink beer all day long.

Beyond the swimming holes and the beer bars, the Hill Country is the domain of the official Texas state mammal, the nine-banded armadillo. An outfit by the name of Apelt Armadillo Farms operated in Comfort, Texas, oddly enough

STATS & FACTS

- With 360,000 square feet under its cast-iron dome, the Texas State Capitol is the biggest state capitol building in the nation, and at 308 feet in height it's nearly twenty feet taller than the United States Capitol. But it is shorter than the Louisiana State Capitol, and the United States Capitol has more floor space.

- The Texas state mammal, the nine-banded armadillo, almost always gives birth to a litter of genetically identical quadruplets derived from a single egg.

- Austin has more music venues per capita than any other major American city.

used armadillo skin in the manufacture of bags and lamps and assorted knickknacks. Armadillo World Headquarters was ground zero for Austin's outlaw country explosion in the 1970s. Sadly, both enterprises have long since shut down, but the armadillo is still lurking in these hills. Please brake for them.

BIG THINGS AND OTHER ROAD ART

Stonehenge II and Easter Island Statues
FM 1340, near Hunt

About 5,000 miles from the original on the Salisbury Plain in England, Stonehenge II is not an enigma. Its mastermind, the late Al Shepperd, started with a single slab of limestone that his neighbor Doug Hill gave to him in 1989. After standing it on

end on his property outside of Hunt, Texas, Shepperd enlisted Hill to build an arch to accentuate it. Then Hill went to town (with Shepperd picking up the tab) and created a three-quarters-scale replica of Stonehenge based on what it originally looked like nearly 4,000 years ago. Aside from the original slab, he didn't use limestone: it seems Stonehenge was easier to re-create with steel frames sheathed in plaster. (It's also easier for bats to roost in the cracks of plaster than those of limestone.) At Shepperd's behest, after Hill finished Stonehenge II, he made a pair of big heads, replicas of the puzzling thirteen-foot statues known as moai on Easter Island. He took one Texas liberty with one of the moai, adding a beer belly that would require a serious regimen of Shiner-lifting if it weren't steel and plaster. Visitors are welcome to check out these masterworks of roadside kitsch during daylight hours.

Read:
- Texas: A Novel by James A. Michener
- The Improbable Rise of Redneck Rock by Jan Reid and Scott Newton
- A Sniper in the Tower: The Charles Whitman Murders by Gary M. Lavergne

Listen:
- Hi, How Are You by Daniel Johnston
- The Psychedelic Sounds of the 13th Floor Elevators by the 13th Floor Elevators
- Viva Terlingua! Live Recording Concert at Luckenbach by Jerry Jeff Walker
- Red Headed Stranger by Willie Nelson

Watch:
- Slacker
- Texas Chainsaw Massacre
- Office Space

To-Do Checklist:
- Cruise Sixth Street
- Seduce a co-ed
- Seduce a lobbyist
- Seduce an armadillo
- For the sake of your family and your political future, don't get caught

Also provoking dumbstruck expressions from passersby in the area, Boot Hill (south of Hunt) is fronted by a fence with posts topped with upside-down boots for a full half mile.

Cathedral of Junk
4422 Lareina Dr., Austin
512-299-7413

Tucked in a nondescript neighborhood on the south side of Austin, this is a house of worship whose prime tenet is planned obsolescence. Vince Hannemann has taken it upon himself to construct a three-story temple out of, well, junk. The mostly donated materials he has incorporated into the structure over the years include engines, action figures, old trophies, wheels, a satellite dish, CDs suspended by strings, street signs, rocking horses, car seats, and pretty much anything else that you might throw away. Hannemann started building the Cathedral of Junk in 1989, and now it dominates pretty much all of his backyard. He opens it to the public from noon to 6 PM on weekends, but if you catch him at home he'll let you climb the precarious staircases and pray at his church made entirely of things that narrowly avoided the landfill.

Pots and Plants's Pink Flamingos
5902 Bee Caves Rd. (at Loop 360)
512-327-4564
www.plasticpinkflamingos.com

On the west side of Austin, a veritable herd of plastic pink flamingos works year-round to lure gardeners and landscapers into Pots and Plants Garden Center. Debuting in 1989, the faux birds soon attracted opposition from stuffy officials, but ultimately won their right to flaunt on the roadside, free from interference from the Man. So they do exactly that.

R.I.P.

James A. Michener, 1907–1997
Austin Memorial Park,
2800 Hancock Dr., Austin

An Austin resident in his autumn years, James Michener told big stories about big places—remarkably researched epics interwoven with the history of Alaska, Colorado, Hawaii, and, of course, Texas. His eponymous book on the Lone Star State

bridges the widely misunderstood gap between the arrival of the Spanish and that fateful morning at the Alamo.

Adopted and raised Quaker, he taught high school English and edited social studies textbooks before he was called to naval duty in World War II. His military stint led to his breakthrough book, *Tales of the South Pacific*, in 1946. About forty books followed, nearly one a year for the next half century. Leaving behind a bibliography 2,500 works long, Michener said he would spend twelve to fifteen hours a day at his typewriter for months on end, weaving his imagination and meticulous research into rich tapestries of historical fiction. His gravestone says it all: James Michener—Traveler, Citizen, Writer. An admirable, perhaps perfect, epitaph.

VICE

Austin Nightlife

One of the best places to catch a buzz and some live music in the whole country, Sixth Street is definitely the drunkest street in Texas. Hippies, hipsters, hip-hoppers, and rednecks converge on the seven blocks between Interstate 35 and Congress Avenue, one of the densest clusters of watering holes and music venues anywhere. The street is often closed to traffic and is user friendly, with minimal cover charges and relatively cheap drinks. Some say it's past its prime, gotten

too much hype for its own good, but it's still a very easy place to accidentally spill half a dozen Shiner Bocks down your throat if you're not careful.

Casino El Camino (517 E. Sixth St., 512-469-9330, www.casinoelcamino.net) is a heavily muraled and gargoyled carnivalesque joint that's the mutant of Sixth Street and known for its three-quarter-pound burgers. Momo's (618 W. Sixth St., 512-479-8848, www.momosclub.com) is a great venue for local and touring acts, seven nights a week, with one of the best decks in Texas. Get your tickets early for movies at the original Alamo Drafthouse Cinema (320 E. Sixth St., 512-476-1320, www.originalalamo.com), where the programming includes kitschy one-nighters and critically acclaimed indie films, and you can wet your whistle before, during, and after the flicks.

Just north of Sixth, amidst a strip of music venues near the Texas State Capitol, the Mohawk (912 Red River Rd., 512-482-8404, www.mohawkaustin.com) is a funky place made from recycled wood and radio towers, featuring some of the best acoustics in town. In the Warehouse District, Antone's (213 W. Fifth St., 512-320-8424, www.antones.net) is one of Austin's stalwart music venues—it was established at a different location in 1975 by the late Clifford Antone—and a great spot for catching a show most nights of the week.

But Austin's nightlife doesn't begin and end downtown. The bar scene here includes an inordinate number of oddball establishments sporting oddball themes. For example, it's always Christmas at Lala's Little Nugget (2207 Justin Ln., 512-453-2521). This strip-mall dive on the north side of town, said to be Quentin Tarantino's favorite bar, is oddly unaware of the season: a string of dangling elves gyrate when the men's room door opens, a Santa mask leers, and a faux tree twinkles, making it easy to feel all drunk and sappy, holiday-style—even in July.

A ramshackle place in the shadow of a gleaming new development, the Mean Eyed Cat (1621 W. Fifth St., 512-472-6326, www.themeaneyedcat.com) is the coolest (and only) Johnny Cash–themed bar where I've drunk a beer. Let's see, there are Cash portraits galore, Cash records nailed to the wall, and a Cash-labeled chainsaw hanging from the rafters (complemented by a framed and autographed Leatherface glossy on the wall). There is also a killer fenced beer garden out front and live music most nights.

The G & S Lounge (2420 S. 1st St., 512-707-8702) features video games, roaming fat dogs, a young, hip crowd, and the locally infamous Beer Nazi, who will cut you off without notice if you're a bad tipper or an otherwise unwanted patron. It looks like hell on the outside, but on the inside it feels like the spawn of a great dive and the coolest, weirdest guy on the block's garage.

Ginny's Little Longhorn Saloon (5434 Burnet Rd., 512-458-1813, www.ginnyslittlelonghorn.com) looks like a dinky chapel, but it's actually a great honky-tonk featuring live music most nights and Chicken Shit Bingo on Sunday afternoons. Chicken Shit Bingo involves a chicken, of course, a bingo board, and the inevitable soiling of the latter.

Then there's the Carousel Lounge (1110 E. 52nd, 512-452-6790), the most dismal circus-themed bar in town, perhaps the world. Clad in murals of clowns and chimps and the like, and sporting an odd gold-speckled carousel with a chicken and a goat on the back bar, the place is located squarely at the intersection of mirthful and depressing. A stone's throw from the interstate in north Austin, this is a favorite of the local punk scene, featuring an odd 3-D pachyderm behind the stage and a similar giraffe standing guard at the door.

And no rundown of Austin nightlife would be complete without mentioning the superlative Continental Club (1315 S. Congress Ave., 512-441-2444, www.continentalclub.com), opening in 1957 and hosting burlesque shows, Stevie Ray Vaughan, and annual Elvis birthday parties in the time since.

Gruene Hall

1281 Gruene Rd., New Braunfels
830-606-1281
www.gruenehall.com

Open since 1878, the Gruene (pro-
nounced like the color) Hall is
the oldest operating dance hall in
Texas. The stage has seen legends
like Willie Nelson, Lyle Lovett, and
George Strait. Long tables at the
front of the room are prime seats
for watching the band, and the
dance floor is in the back. The bar
is behind the stage in a separate room, its walls clad in the
glossies of the many music legends who have taken the stage
over the venue's 130-plus years of existence.

Avocado Margaritas at Curra's Grill

614 E. Oltorf St., Austin
512-444-0012
www.currasgrill.com

An avocado margarita—I know it sounds awful on paper, but
I know firsthand that it tastes great in real life. Somehow the
masterminds behind the bar at Curra's have figured out how
to take an avocado and add creamy deliciousness to lime and
tequila. Don't try this at home.

Luckenbach

A short drive from Fredericksburg
www.luckenbachtexas.com

The late John Russell "Hondo" Crouch is a Texas legend.
The right-wing writer, swimmer, goat farmer, and humorist
bought the town of Luckenbach in 1971 so he would have a
place to drink beer. Declaring himself mayor of the dinky
town—originally founded as an Indian trading post by

German immigrant Jacob Luckenbach in 1849—Crouch set to work establishing as many wacky traditions as he could come up with, including women-only chili cook-offs and no-talent contests. The outdoor stage emerged as a favorite venue of Willie Nelson, Jerry Jeff Walker, Waylon Jennings, and other legends.

Still centered on the old general store, Luckenbach remains one of the best places to catch live music in all of Texas, with some good grub and ice-cold Shiner to boot. Hondo, who died of a heart attack soon after spearheading the Non-Buy Centennial against the commercialization of the Bicentennial of the Declaration of Independence in 1976, is memorialized out front.

Arkey Blue's Silver Dollar Bar
308 Main St., Bandera
830-796-8826

The best honky-tonk in the self-proclaimed Cowboy Capital of the World, Arkey's opened in a Bandera basement in the 1940s and hasn't changed much over the years. Its floors are still covered in sawdust, the beer is still cold, and the music is still as old school as Texas country gets.

STAR MAPS

- The *Texas Chainsaw Massacre* was shot on location in Austin, Round Rock, and Bastrop in 1973. The family's house was moved from Austin to Kingsland in 1998. Shot on a budget of $140,000, the prototype slasher flick ultimately grossed more than $30 million domestically.

- While many of the prominent locations shot in Richard Linklater's seminal indie flick *Slacker* no longer exist, some do live on: the East MLK Bridge (where the typewriter is chucked into the river), the Second Street Warehouse District (where Madonna's Pap smear enters the picture), and Mount Bonnell (the location of the final scene where a Super-8 is chucked into Lake Austin).

- In 1993, manic-depressive musical genius Daniel Johnston painted a mural on the southern wall of the former Sound Exchange at 2100 Guadalupe Street. The image first appeared on his *Hi, How Are You* album (a.k.a. *Jeremiah the Innocent*).

- The South Austin Museum of Popular Culture (1516 S. Lamar, Austin, 512-440-8318, www.sampoc.org) is the local repository of rock-poster art that has graced the city's store-fronts and bulletin boards. The museum is open Thursday through Saturday, or by appointment.

HUH?

Museum of the Weird

412 E. 6th St., Austin
(in the back of Lucky Lizard Curios & Gifts)
512-476-5493
www.museumoftheweird.com

It's hard to pass up any museum with displays on Texas Bigfoot, a Feejee Mermaid, and two-headed livestock, no matter how lacking the collection otherwise might be. And while the inventory of weirdness might be a bit limited for the price of admission, you've got to expect to pay a little something if you want to see pretty much any shrunken heads, no?

Wilson House of Laminates

(tours available by appointment)
1714 S. 61st St., Temple
800-433-3222
www.wilsonart.com

The founder of the decorative laminate giant now known as Wilsonart, Ralph Wilson Sr. wanted his house to showcase his company's plastic laminates, so he covered nearly every surface at his home in Temple with laminates of every description and hue. The place served as a model home and a field lab for the company, and residence for Wilson and his wife, Sunny. On most of the house's walls there is no drywall, just heavy-duty laminates on top of two-by-fours. Wilson's house is now on the National Register of Historic Places and is certainly one of the most plastic-heavy joints on the whole list.

Kimble County Monster: The Texas Werewolf?
Kimble County

Among Texas's lesser-known cryptozoological enigmas is the alleged werewolf who prowls the Hill Country under the light of full moons in search of Shiner Bock and livestock. Keep your eyes peeled for a wolf at the bar in bloody overalls and a cowboy hat.

Museum of Natural & Artificial Ephemerata
1808 Singleton, Austin
www.mnae.org

Tucked away in an east Austin neighborhood, this museum's impermanent collection covers a wide range of off-kilter objects in five categories: naturalia and artificialia; urban phantasmago-ria; celebrity; snow globes; and, of course, sleep. Even more impermanent exhibitions have covered everything from monstrosities to wondrous instruments and will almost certainly continue to broaden in scope. The museum is typically open on Saturdays only.

GRUB

Breakfast Tacos

Available all over Austin—including the Spider House Patio Bar & Cafe (2908 Fruth St., 512-480-9562, www.spiderhousecafe .com), Tamale House (5003 Airport Blvd., 512-453-9842), and Juan in a Million (2300 E. Cesar Chavez St., 512-472-3872, www .juaninamillion.com)—breakfast tacos aren't just for breakfast in these parts. They're also great for lunch or dinner or a snack in between breakfast and lunch or else between lunch and dinner. Or after dinner. Better yet, after a long night of drinking. In fact, give me eggs and salsa on a tortilla and I think I may be able to rally from my stupor and continue drinking for a couple more hours.

Kolaches
Hill Country, festival in Caldwell, Fayetteville (self-proclaimed Kolache Capital of Texas)

Kolaches are sweet little rolls stuffed with pretty much anything. You never know if it's going to be fruit or meat, or cheese or spinach—well, not unless you poke your finger into the middle before you bite. Kolaches are like donuts and are widely available and often purchased by the dozen in the Hill Country. In fact, there are numerous "kolaches and donuts" places that won't bat an eyelash if you mix and match sausage and jalapeño kolaches with lemon jellies and Boston cremes.

Kreuz Market
619 N. Colorado St., Lockhart
512-398-2361
www.kreuzmarket.com

One of the true temples of Texas barbecue, Kreuz Market is the authentic article. Their slow-cooked brisket—get it fat—tastes like it's undergone some sort of time-honored culinary alchemy. At the first counter, they sell their brisket, ribs, and sausage by the pound, wrapped in wax paper. Get it and walk into the next room. Act like you know what you're doing. At the second counter, order your drinks and sides: hunks of cheese, interestingly, also by the pound, and kraut, beans, and German potatoes by the pint, quart, or gallon.

In business since 1900, Kreuz relocated from its long-time downtown location to new majestic brick digs on the north side of town in 1999, and a relative operates the old place as Smitty's. A sign at the entrance of the new Kreuz explains the house policies: No barbecue sauce (Nothing to hide). No forks (They are at the end of your arms). No salads (Remember, no forks). No credit cards (Bank doesn't sell barbecue). No kidding (See owner's face). Just the best barbecue and sausage we can make.

Oatmeal, Texas

Few people know oatmeal consists of ground oat groats. Even fewer people know what an oat groat is. But if you are one of these people, this is your kind of town. As its name suggests, Oatmeal (pop. 20) is a true mecca for Wilford Brimley disciples everywhere, hosting the annual Oatmeal Festival every Labor Day weekend. Plus the stuff is used in cookies as well as stout beer, so it's got to be good.

Blue Bell Ice Cream
1101 Blue Bell Rd, Brenham
800-327-8135
www.bluebell.com

Blue Bell Creameries has been cranking out its fiendishly addictive ice cream for nearly a century. Using milk, cream, sugar, and assorted ingredients, Blue Bell sells half gallons of a few dozen flavors at any given time, including the best-selling Homemade Vanilla. Tours of its production facilities in Brenham are offered for $3, which includes a gateway cup of ice cream to get you hooked.

SLEEPS

Austin

It would be difficult to find a more pro-totypically vintage motel than the 1938 Austin Motel (1220 S. Congress Ave., 512-441-1157, www.austinmotel.com). Hipper and pricier, the Hotel San Jose (1316 S. Congress Ave., 800-574-8897, www.sanjosehotel.com) is from the same era as the Austin Motel, but it got a colorful contemporary facelift in the 1990s, catalyzing the entire neighborhood.

Hangar Hotel
155 Airport Rd., Fredericksburg
830-997-9990
www.hangarhotel.com

If you've always wanted to sleep in an airplane hangar, without all of those pesky airplanes, this is your place. Located at the Gillespie County Airport, the hotel is modeled after a World War II hangar, with an observation deck and a bar right on the runway.

MISC.

World's Largest Urban Bat Colony
Under the Congress Avenue Bridge, Austin

The most populous urban bat colony on the planet is right under the Congress Avenue Bridge, but it hasn't always been a flying-mammal hot spot. When the bridge's deck was beefed up in 1980, the new design featured crevasses about an inch wide and sixteen inches deep—collectively the perfect size and temperature for a breeding ground for 750,000 Mexican free-tailed bats. So they show up en masse to breed year after year, from March to November.

Toy Joy
2900 Guadalupe St., Austin
512-320-0090
www.toyjoy.com

I picked up a couple of rubber octopi at this great, proudly odd toy store near the University of Texas campus, and you should too. Why wouldn't you? Huh? No way. That's not a good reason at all. Keep in mind there is a plethora of non-octopus toys, including but not limited to stuffed monkeys, rubber duckies, Superman knickknacks, and action figures galore.

Barton Springs Pool
In Zilker Park, 2101 Barton Springs Rd., Austin
512-476-9044

There may be no better place in the world on a hot summer afternoon than the Barton Springs Pool. Fed by springs that pump out sixty-eight-degree water year-round and surrounded by verdant and shady slopes, this is Austin's truly sacred place. This is also where Robert Redford learned to swim and one of the very few places you might encounter the endangered Barton Springs salamander.

River Tubing, Rafting, and Carousing
New Braunfels and San Marcos
www.tubetexas.com

The Hill Country is home to some of the world's most idyllic waters to meander in inflated plastic, a beer in hand. Come summer, the rivers are the place to be, most notably the popular Guadalupe, the clear San Marcos, the cool Frio, and the short Comal. Outfitters in New Braunfels and San Marcos will gladly set you up with rental tubes and other necessities. (Yes, beer is considered a necessity by serious tubers.) Booze is not banned outright on any of the rivers, but glass and Styrofoam are big no-nos.

LONE ROCKSTAR TOUR

5 DAYS, 500 MILES, 126 SONGS (GIVE OR TAKE)

I'm about ten miles outside of Turkey, Texas, hometown of the late, great Bob Wills, king of Western swing. I'm listening to his expert fiddling with the Texas Playboys, as the wrinkled landscape alternates between gold and green and red.

Then I'm at a stop sign. Next to it is another sign welcoming me to town. Turkey, Texas, is spelled out in black metal. Home of Bob Wills. There is a water tower and a small downtown built of brick, surrounded by a rough grid equally populated by houses and scrub.

One of the few paved streets in this dinky Panhandle town leads to the Bob Wills Community Center, home to a medical clinic and the Bob Wills Museum.

I pass the museum door for the bathroom. *Just like a good song, I can't be rushed,* I think as I pee. I wash my hands and dry them on my jeans.

Back in the hallway, the museum door is locked. I hear someone in the clinic, so I wander in and find a guy buried beyond his shoulders in a refrigerator, rummaging around.

"Is the museum open?" I ask.

The fridge disgorges a bearded and bespectacled guy.

"There was a funeral," he drawls. "Hold on. I'll open it up for ya."

He leaves me to my own devices in the hall for a few minutes, then lets me in and turns on the fluorescents. He introduces himself as Don Turner, who runs the clinic. I ask him about Wills and his legacy.

"He had a different style," Turner answers. "Even The Beatles were influenced by him. It wasn't so much the music as the way he wrote music." He tells me how he infused Western music with jazz guitar. "Country was just three chords, verse, chorus, verse, chorus. He changed the way music was written. He got into the Rock and Roll Hall of Fame. That says a lot."

Don shuffles back across the hall to the clinic. "Let me know when you're done."

I peruse the black-and-white photos, the letters, awards, clippings, instruments, and mementos (including stage clothing, two trademark cigar holders, and an antique portable phonograph with a Texas-shaped record on it).

Wills first broke into show business at age nine, after he hopped on stage to replace his wayward father in 1914. He first made it on the radio with the unfortunately named Light Crust Doughboys in 1929. According to various bits of information on the walls, he made dozens of hit records and Hollywood movies before he passed away in 1975.

A state record

. . . . .

Driving on to Lubbock, with Johnny Cash's *Live at San Quentin* blaring through the speakers, "A Boy Named Sue" comes on.

Crop dusters dart above the fields on either side of the blacktop. I see a dead porcupine, a live coyote, huge farm machines and tractors, and big bales of hay on the side of the road. Stray cotton balls line the roadside, occasionally drifting onto the asphalt.

Swapping Cash for Sabbath somewhere around Floydada, I get to Lubbock before sundown and meet Ryan, with the local tourism bureau, for dinner in the Depot District. We talk about Buddy Holly almost immediately. He tells me

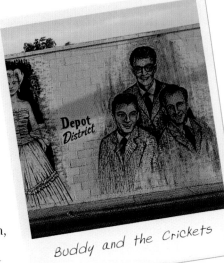

Buddy and the Crickets

he went to the same elementary, middle, and high schools as Holly, although about fifty years later.

"Someone who starts here and plays in the small bars, you never know where he's going to end up," Ryan says. "FYI, he died when he was twenty-two—what were you doing when you were twenty-two?" Not much, I say to myself.

He tells me he DJs at local clubs and plays drums and guitar in a local band called Hollowed Out. I tell him about my band Weird Al Qaida. "It's a release from day-to-day life. It's not one of those things where we think we're going to make it big and sell a ton of CDs. It's an escape from reality."

I couldn't agree with him more.

Later I ask Ryan why the Lubbock area has proven to be such a fertile musical hotbed.

"If you're stuck on a deserted island, are you gonna make the best of it or are you gonna bitch and complain?" he answers.

Later, he mentions that Buddy Holly only used three chords. "John Lennon said, 'Yeah, but he took those three chords and made so many different songs.' You can trace musical influences only so far back until reaching a true innovator," Ryan adds. "Somewhere it's got to stop—when people say, 'We've never heard this kind of music before.'"

After arranging to meet Ryan at a bar on the south side of town later, I make my way over to the Buddy Holly statue and the Lubbock Walk of Fame. Several police cars race by, their sirens wailing, and stop at a nearby motel.

Buddy in bronze

I do a counterclockwise lap around Buddy's statue, aglow in streetlight. The names on the plaques that ring the statue's base include some big ones, all with roots in the Texas Panhandle: Tanya Tucker, Mac Davis, Waylon Jennings, Bob Wills, and the great Roy Orbison.

Orbison grew up in Wink, a speck of a town near the Monahans Sandhills, southwest of Lubbock. Along with Holly, he made it okay to be a geek *and* a rocker. His askew eyes, always hidden by black sunglasses, were certainly questioned by marketers looking to move records with good looks, but—like Holly—his undeniable talent defied the music industry's bias against human imperfection.

Also on the Walk of Fame: Barry Corbin, the actor who played the general in *WarGames* and the old man in *No Country for Old Men*. His plaque makes me think of a song I wrote about Lubbock for my former band, The Barrys, called "Piss on a Sparkplug."

I'd piss on a sparkplug if it'd do any good
Siftin' through garbage, searching for gold
I'd run up the ramp to the sweet pie in the sky
Sippin' free bourbon, bathin' in wine

Take us down
Take us down
Take us down
Take us down to defcon three
Exactly where we want to be

Bobby and Buddy and Barry
Prairie dogs in Mackenzie Park
I'm goin' down that old lonesome road, babe
Fuck, ma, caught in a shitstorm again

Take us down
Take us down
Take us down
Take us down to defcon two
We'll know what we want to do

At a bar called the Gas Light later that night, I meet Ryan and his friends Erica and Erin to watch another friend, Chase Tutor, perform. A singer-songwriter with an acoustic guitar, Tutor mainly strums through originals, throwing in the occasional cover to keep the crowd happy.

In between sets, he comes over to our table. A study in contrasts, scruffy with a glass of red wine and perhaps a bit buzzed, Tutor says Lubbock is a great town for musicians. "I don't have to have a day job here," he says, noting that he pays the bills by gigging four or five nights a week and that gigs pay better than they do in Austin. "There are too many musicians there," he says. (He also calls Lubbock "the armpit of Texas." I disagree: I've always thought of Lubbock as Texas's elbow.)

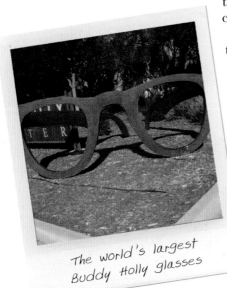

The world's largest
Buddy Holly glasses

The good thing about not having a day job is you can focus on songwriting and music. The bad thing about not having a day job is that it's pretty easy to party full time.

I go back to my hotel about 1 AM and sleep fitfully until 8 AM.

I make my way to the Buddy Holly Center for a look at Buddy's old Cub Scout uniform, his guns, his records, his letters, his guitars, and, of course, his glasses—his only possession recovered from the crash site after his death on February 2, 1959.

A display on the history of rock includes a line from *Rolling Stone Illustrated History of Rock & Roll.* "Rock and roll was an inevitable outgrowth of the social and musical interaction between blacks and whites in the South and Southwest." The accompanying timeline highlights Bob Wills's refusal to let the Grand Ole Opry hide his drummer with a curtain in 1944.

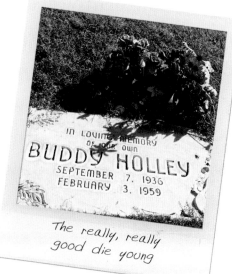

In Loving Memory Of Our Own
BUDDY HOLLEY
SEPTEMBER 7. 1936
FEBRUARY 3. 1959

The really, really good die young

After learning standards by Hank Williams, Bill Monroe, and other country legends, Holly was a virtuoso guitarist, banjo player, and mandolinist by the time he was fifteen. As he wrote in an essay for high school, "I have a thought of making a career out of Western music, but I will just have to wait and see how that turns out."

It turned out really well. In 1955, Elvis Presley came to Lubbock, and his performances changed Holly's musical direction. Two years later, after a slow start, "That'll Be the Day" sold over a million units in its first four months, slowly working its way to the top of the Billboard chart by September 1957.

By early 1958, Holly was a certified international phenomenon, a critical darling, and a commercial success. All of Holly's hard work leading to his success was an example of

the American dream, a display argues. But it doesn't mention that his death at age twenty-two was just the opposite.

Before leaving Lubbock in my rearview mirror, I make one last stop on the east side of town: Buddy's grave at Lubbock Cemetery. I leave a million-yen note I found in San Francisco nine months ago, placing a nickel on top of it to keep it from flickering away in the wind. It joins a collection of guitar picks, coins, flowers, stuffed animals, and a toy car.

A deep breath later, I'm off on the five-hour drive to the Hill Country. On the way, the music of many of Texas's musical superstars comes over the Saturn's tinny speakers: Janis Joplin, Steve Earle, the Butthole Surfers, Lyle Lovett…

· · · · ·

I arrive at the Lazy T, just outside of town, around 6 PM and make a quick turn to downtown Fredericksburg. People adjourning from a wine festival in the middle of town are alternately happy and loud. The sidewalks are full of all sorts of people, mostly Texans, and shopkeepers are shutting down their colorful stores made of limestone bricks and well-stocked with Texan décor, Texan candy (i.e., jalapeño brittle and Texas-sized jelly beans), and Texan knickknacks.

I settle at Hondo's for a Shiner Black and chicken enchiladas, served in a tin bowl. But tonight's band is nowhere to be found. Rumor has it they forgot about the Hondo's gig and are currently playing another show in Austin. The staff works the phones to find a local picker to take to the outdoor stage.

A night at Hondo's

After dinner, I look at the shelves with Hondo's T-shirts and ballcaps, cactus backscratchers, and a few books. I leaf through *Hondo: My Father* and learn about the late Hondo Crouch, clown prince of nearby Luckenbach and this joint's namesake, and his varied attempts for his one-person town's secession and other hijinks. Next to the books is a letter written by Willie Nelson after Hondo's 1976 passing, memorializing him as a legend of Texas eccentricity.

With the band nowhere to be found, I stroll back east on Main Street. A poster advertising the intriguingly named Mighty Orq—and no cover—lures me to the Auslander Biergarten, one of several *biergartens* in town, thanks to its founding by German immigrants in the 1840s.

On the way, I catch the strains of blues guitar on the shadowy block north and detour to find a chubby Hispanic guy channeling Stevie Ray Vaughan at an outdoor bar. "I'm walking the tightrope," he wails above the twangy snarl of his guitar.

I continue my counterclockwise lap around the block and hear the strains of the Mighty Orq through the darkness and soon am plopping down at the Auslander's bar. The band offers a hearty helping of Texas blues rock, with a side of funky soul.

The place comes alive when the Orq rips into a stellar cover of Prince's "Kiss." The tune transcends the crowd's differences. People get up and dance—one guy in a cowboy hat starts enthusiastically doing his own interpretation of the raise-the-roof jig.

Fiddles seeking fiddlers

Two Shiners and a long drive weighing on my eyelids, I make one last stop at Hondo's, where they in

fact pulled in a couple local pickers to play for the night. A happy drunken quartet slow dances with one another.

It's time for bed.

. . . . .

The next morning, I'm watching a local news story from Austin about the closing of a popular music venue, The Backyard, because of development pressure. "It used to be nothing but woods out here," says one source. "Now it's surrounded by shopping malls."The next story is about recycling. "It would only cost us $1.77 a month to throw less away and consume less," says the pro-recycling point person.

Whether the product is music or trash, it seems our economy has run roughshod over our culture for quite some time.

A few minutes later, I'm strolling around downtown Fredericksburg, checking out the selection of doodads and hot sauces and assorted Texas schwag, and the fiddles and the kazoos and the spoons at Hill Country Music.

Then I drive to Luckenbach (pop. 3), Hondo Crouch's ramshackle town of weathered wood, license plates, and ice-cold Shiner. There is a benefit to help rebuild the Old Quarter Acoustic Cafe in Galveston, destroyed by Hurricane Ike. An acoustic duo plays on the outdoor stage, where the outstretched limbs of a magnificent oak shade the picnic tables populated by a mix of Texas hippies, cowboys, and bikers. The diverse, albeit predominately white, crowd is connected through the shared experience of listening to the "stories," as the second songstress puts it, sung by those on the stage.

The sky is blue and puffy white, the weather is warm, and a slight breeze meanders through the green hills. I sip on a bottle of Shiner Bock and listen to her voice, soft but full of flinty twang, and strumming that carries through the thick Hill Country air.

Later I peruse the Luckenbach gift shop and read more about Hondo Crouch and some of his reprinted writing in a

publication with the music calendar. In his column in a local paper, "Cedar Creek Clippings," the right-leaning Crouch satirized the easy corruption of politics through the fictional town and characters of Cedar Creek. In 1971, he bought his very own Cedar Creek in the form of Luckenbach, an abandoned 1840s town, and proceeded to stage all sorts of events—no-talent contests, women-only chili cook-offs, and mud-dauber celebrations. He died a few months after protesting the commercialization of the Declaration of Independence in the bicentennial year of 1976.

Well-known Hill Country singer-songwriter Gary P. Nunn, formerly of Jerry Jeff Walker's backing band, is next on the stage. He gets the crowd involved in a few sing-alongs before launching into his trademark "London Homesick Blues," the theme song for the *Austin City Limits* TV show.

"I want to go home with the armadillo," he sings. "Good country music from Amarillo and Abilene, the friendliest people and the prettiest women you've ever seen."

The crowd smiles and sings along. I get a feeling, all warm, peaceful, and easy, wishing I could stay here all day.

But I've got to check out Stonehenge II and there is no time like the present.

I play the CD of another Texas original, Daniel Johnston, on my car stereo on the half-hour drive. "I had this dream the other night," he caterwauls. "It was really weird, they were playing guitars, and getting loud, and they spilt beer on Jesus. I save cigarette butts for a poor girl across town…"

There are bugs in the meadow and buzzards in the sky and bats squeaking in the cracks of Stonehenge II. The Hill Country's replica enigma is flanked by a pair of reproduced Easter Island statues, and I duck the sun in the shade of one for a few peaceful minutes.

· · · · ·

After zipping back to Fredericksburg, I check in at the Hangar Hotel, a hangar at the airport converted into a cool lodging, and then head out for dinner. The brewery closed at 7 PM, I learn at

7:45, so I soon find myself in the courtyard at Hondo's, hunched over a Shiner and portobello mushroom quesadillas.

The same pickers are on the gazebo stage. "I started at the bottom," sings one, "and I'm working my way down."

Then they get all right-wing on me and sing Hillary Clinton a sarcastic happy birthday.

"Blaaaah," comes out of my mouth, some sort of uncontrollable reflex.

Politics and music don't mix—unless, of course, you agree with the politics in question. Then again, I can't see why a talented Democrat musician couldn't collaborate with a talented Republican musician. Only it doesn't seem like it happens all that often.

And at that, I call it a night.

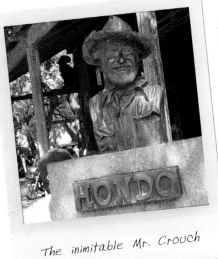

The inimitable Mr. Crouch

· · · · ·

Before leaving the Hangar Hotel, I have coffee and watch *The Today Show*. A guy named Patrick Henry Hughes, born blind and seated in a wheelchair, talks to Meredith Vieira about overcoming obstacles before playing "Somewhere Over the Rainbow" on the piano and belting it out with more than a little passion for the music. It is a good foot on which to start the day.

I work my way north to Llano, and east to Oatmeal, then southeast to Austin. The drive is beautiful, a gentle undulation swathed in the green shag of trees and prickly pears. The music on the radio creates a wide spectrum from MC Hammer's "U Can't Touch This" to The Beatles's "A Day in the Life." I don't know if any two smash-hit songs could be more unequal in terms of the talent that went into their creation.

I make it to Austin in time for a late lunch. After a stint at a South Congress coffee shop, I make a whirlwind sightseeing loop from the Cathedral of Junk to Toy Joy

to James Michener's gravesite to Ginny's Little Longhorn Saloon. From Ginny's, I call Thomas, a local music journalist and graduate student who agreed to let me stay on the futon at his and his girlfriend Starla's place in east Austin. (I'd registered with CouchSurfing.org before I left.)

Thomas and Starla are out front with their excitable mutt, Willis, as I pull up to their house. After introductions, Thomas and Willis and I head over to the corner store for a six-pack, then return to their kitchen table for beer and beef stew.

Seeing a Casio keyboard atop Willis's kennel, I tell them about Weird Al Qaida, my recently defunct experimental psychedelic electronic punk band.

"What did you play?" Thomas asks.

"Keyboards," I respond. "And I sing. But my keyboards are really just a layer of psychedelic noise. I don't play too many melodies." I point to the Casio. "Do you play?"

Thomas looks at the keyboard and smiles. "No, but I did learn how to play Cyndi Lauper's 'Time After Time' the other day," he replies. "Starla's learning how to play guitar."

Starla meanwhile is wandering the house. "The door is open," she suddenly shouts, "and the dog is gone!"

All of ten seconds later, the three of us are in the street trying to corral the awkward but agile one-year-old terrier mix. Starla attempts to lure Willis with the stew-

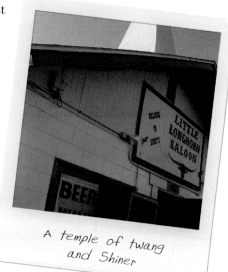

A temple of twang and Shiner

serving spoon, but it's Thomas who has to apply a football-style tackle to finally nab him.

Back inside, I learn Starla works as a school social worker and Thomas is a freelance music writer focused on hip-hop, soul, and funk for the weekly *The Austin Chronicle* as he finishes dual master's degrees in Latin

studies and journalism. He talks about a couch-surfing trip he took via CouchSurfing.com. "I did a figure eight around Texas," he says, describing a night straight out of a horror movie in swampy East Texas.

Starla's brother Tyson shows up for a bowl of stew, and with Halloween looming later in the week, costumes are discussed. Tyson is going to be the Incredible Hulk. His friend is going to be Slim Goodbody. Starla says she is going to be a purple people eater—mostly because she has a lot of purple in her closet. "I just need an eye, a horn, and some wings."

I tell Thomas I used to write about music for Denver's alt-weekly, *Westword*. "Writing about music, as they say, can be like dancing about architecture," I say. "It's easy to get caught up in clichés."

"It gets easier," he replies, adding that he also does radio pieces for a local NPR show, *Texas Music Matters*. "With radio, you have a whole different palette to work with."

Thomas also hosts a college-radio show called *The Afro-boogaloo Soul Revue* as Rev Get Down, and his time slot is fast approaching. I tell him my musical journey across Texas has been especially Caucasian thus far and tag along with him to the station.

In a funky studio bedecked with a rubber chicken and a picture of KVRX "founder" Ronald Reagan, Rev Get Down begins to spin an hour of vintage and contemporary funk and soul gems from near and far. He starts with the Magic Circle Express's "Magic Fever" before playing dirty old Andre Williams's "Humpin', Bumpin', and Thumpin'," a cover of "I Put a Spell On You" by The Animals, and a catchy psychedelic soul number by Shuggie Otis, "Sweet Thang."

At one point, Thomas passes me a CD by Steam Heat, a funk outfit based out of Austin in the 1970s. "They were doing funk when Austin was all about outlaw country, so they were cutting against the grain," he says. "And they were one of Austin's first integrated bands and one of the first bands to play for integrated crowds on Austin's west side."

It strikes me that if rock and roll was an inevitable result of interracial interaction, and since integrated audiences that began with Ray Charles and continued with Steam Heat had progressed to white suburban kids embracing black hip-hop artists, then the crossover had come full circle by the emergence of Eminem. Where do we go from here?

How about a Portuguese version of Michael Jackson's "Thriller" by a Brazilian pop singer? "It's pretty much my favorite song ever," Thomas laughs. "The chorus makes no sense in English or Portuguese."

"Criser!" the vocalist wails. "Take it ease!"

He may be linguistically in left field, but he more than compensates with his enthusiasm.

Thomas finishes the night's revue with a song by the Gerson King Combo, a Brazilian funk band that he describes as obsessed with James Brown.

We head to an east Austin watering hole, the Longbranch Inn, replete with mounted ungulate heads with flowers in their horns. It turns out Thomas is working on a final project for his master's detailing the emergence of 1970s Brazilian funk and its sociopolitical implications.

"I like it when music is bigger than music," he says.

I agree. Music journalism is not as cliché-ridden when the subject is bigger than music, and truths and ideas can bounce around the world on the wings of great songs.

Deep West Texas, pyramid of flames
Where the river bends slow but the river bends big
The sky is alive with the Milky Way
Psychedelic cactus juice, I take a swig

Sweet desert nectar
Flames lick my aura
Musk and rumble in the yucca
'twas a triple-tongued javelina

—from the Weird Al Qaida non-hit
"Three-Tongued Desert Pig"

After a night on the futon in the corner of Starla and Thomas's kitchen, I wake to read Tuesday's *Chronicle* headline: "Austin's weirdness is compromised now that the city's been monetized." The column, however, complains more about non-weird things like golf courses and dry cleaners going the way of the dodo, not extinctions of authentically weird landmarks like the Cathedral of Junk.

Willis!

Before I head out to explore Austin for the day, Willis and Thomas and I head to the dog park on Town Lake on the west side of town. En route, with Daniel Johnston playing on my car stereo, Thomas tells me that Johnston is one of the true icons of Austin's music scene, along with Willie Nelson, Stevie Ray Vaughan, Roky Erickson, and Townes Van Zandt.

Long, lean, and shaggy, with inky black hair, upturned ears, and wide, wild eyes, Willis has a blast at the dog park and rests for most of the drive back east.

Thomas needs to write a few album reviews and blurbs about bands and Willis wants to gnaw on my arm, so I leave both of them to their own devices and head to a coffee shop.

On the way, a car pulls up next to me at a red light. Remarkably loud thrash metal oozes from the slightly ajar passenger window. The singer shrieks and growls even less intelligibly than the Brazilian Michael Jackson. It's truly awful.

Some people—including, at times, myself—enjoy driving around and using loud and odd or abrasive music as a badge of honor and/or a bludgeon. The polar opposite of a shared musical experience, this is a good way to drive others away.

The day goes quickly. After drinking coffee and writing for a few hours, I drive around south Austin's side streets. A gray-haired hippie woman slowly walks downhill and a gray-haired hippie man is working his way uphill a couple of blocks away. Half-built houses are next to new eco-mansions next to funky peacocklike houses fronted by colorful baubles and plenty of plant life. All things considered, Austin still feels pretty weird to me.

The man in light

I park on the south side of Town Lake and take off on a walking tour of the city center. The statue of Stevie Ray Vaughan is already accompanied by three tourists and their cameras. Passing it up, I instead cross the First Street Bridge over the lake and make my way up Guadalupe to the googly-eyed bullfrog spray painted on the side of a building near the UT campus.

I am the only one photographing this lesser-known Austin musical landmark.

I worm my way through the student hordes on campus and head back south to Sixth Street downtown for a visit to the Museum of the Weird and a cold Shiner Bock at the Casino El Camino. Before heading back to east Austin, I make one more Shiner stop at the shrine to Johnny Cash that is the Mean Eyed Cat.

Back at my couch-surfing base, Starla wrestles Willis as Thomas tries to work on a story for the *Chronicle*, a short profile of rapper Kool Keith, a.k.a. Dr. Octagon, slated to play an upcoming festival in town.

"I'm actually kind of worried about him," says Thomas. He tells me the interview went on for an hour—and for forty minutes after he stopped his tape recorder. The conversation sashayed from women's lingerie to the lack of streets in modern America to his declining treatment by record execs. Thomas's favorite quote: "Just because you're underground doesn't mean you got to eat baloney sandwiches."

We talk about the Keep Austin Weird coalition.

"Most of the people wearing those T-shirts aren't very weird," says Starla.

"Isn't it just an association for local businesses to fight national chains?" I ask. "I mean, it's not like the muffler guy is going to be that weird."

"Umm, well, we have Rasta Jah Muffler," she retorts. "And Groovy Lube. I went there for an oil change once."

"Were the guys weird?"

"They seemed like they were stoned."

After showering, I go out for a bite to eat and end up nursing another beer at Lala's on the north side of town. But no amount of cold Shiner can motivate me to close down the bats. My lack of energy concludes in a U-turn on Red River and a quick surrender to Thomas and Starla's futon a little after midnight.

· · · · ·

In the morning, I hang out at a coffee shop before heading to Pots and Plants's horde of pink flamingos west of town. Afterward, midday traffic increases my blood pressure just as my radio tunes in Roy Orbison's "Crying." Transfixed by the song, my mind clears.

I continue wandering: an early lunch of kolaches, a visit to the Bob Bullock Texas State History Museum, and a late lunch of breakfast tacos at the Spider House. I have a happy-hour Shiner at the saddest circus-themed bar in Austin, the Carousel Lounge, and then snake my way through rush hour back to east Austin.

Later, Starla, Thomas, and I have avocado margaritas and a groovy Mexican dinner at Curra's, then a drink at the G & S Lounge. Starla calls it a night, but Thomas and I keep up the good fight and head to see the great Maceo Parker, James Brown's onetime sax player, at the legendary downtown nightspot Antone's.

We catch the last three songs. With Maceo at the helm, they last forty-five minutes. He alternates between passionate vocals—he must sing the phrase, "We love you," a thousand times—and virtuosic squawks on his horn. He smiles widely. The band is masterful, rich horns, funky bass, rhythmic drums.

The crowd is happy, the band is happy, the staff is happy.

Maceo leaves the stage around midnight. On the drive home, I ask Thomas how he got into soul and funk, particularly soul and funk from other countries. He tells me that he unearthed James Brown in his dad's record collection as a kid, but it was his discovery of Afrobeat legend Fela Kuti that hooked him for life. "From the second I heard his whole African interpretation of James Brown, I was obsessed."

Like most things in this universe, it's the transition zones that matter, and with music, it's the transition zones between multiple musical grounds that prove the most fertile. As in Bob Wills melding jazz and Western. Or Buddy Holly taking Wills's style and fusing it with nascent rock and roll, or The Beatles taking their cues from Wills and Holly and ultimately LSD, or Dylan and Cash straddling folk and rock and country.

My own musical experimentation has taken a backseat to my writing and traveling. The Barrys's last show was more than five years ago. Weird Al Qaida fell victim to an argument between Duff (bass) and Ingvald (guitar).

My keyboard and microphone have been collecting dust. I haven't written a new song in the better part of a year. I tried to write a country song on a trip to Nashville, but only came up with one good line: "She said that she loved love, but she didn't love lovin' me."

My third and final sleep on the futon ends when Willis pays me a visit early in the morning.

I shake Thomas's hand and hug Starla and scratch Willis, who gently bites me in response, thank them for their hospitality, then make my way out of Austin.

After a barbecue lunch in Lockhart, I loop east to Shiner for a visit to the Spoetzl Brewery, the home of Shiner Bock, but return to the Hill Country for a final night in the idyllic town of Gruene. The restored German village above the Guadalupe River is well known as the home of the oldest dance hall in Texas, Gruene Hall, established in 1878 and still packing them in.

My esteemed hosts

After dinner, I head into the hall for the free show. The place isn't packed, but there are maybe one hundred people sitting on the long benches on the tables nearest the stage, and a few couples dancing on the floor in the rear of the room. An old wooden sign for Nuevo Laredo, Mex., hangs above the arch separating the hall from the bar.

A bartendress wearing Mickey Mouse ears and short shorts is a whirling dervish, serving beers and collecting bottles. A frame on the wall touts the stage being graced by two rock-and-roll hall of famers, Bo Diddley and Jerry Lee Lewis, and the black-and-white publicity stills on the walls include such names as Kris Kristofferson, Lyle Lovett, Los Lobos, Keb' Mo', and Garth Brooks.

This night on the stage, a band named Texas Renegade plays reasonably good country-tinged rock. The harmonica player is incredible—is that "Blister in the Sun" he's riffing on during his solo?—and so are the acoustics, the sound warmly echoing off the timeworn wood.

I need to get back into music. I need to write a new song.

The band plays Dylan's "Like a Rolling Stone" and gets plenty of applause, but it's their finale that really gets the old floorboards humming. "Do it!" hollers an enthusiastic female fan. And the band indeed does it, a bluegrassesque cover of the Divinyls's ode to masturbation, "I Touch Myself." The place goes nuts.

You just never know what will make the masses happy.

Author's note: Following the trip,
Weird Al Qaida finally reunited
after a six-month layoff. Rock and roll.

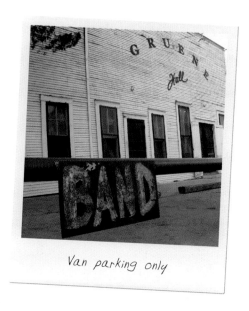

Van parking only

Where to go...

Bob Wills Museum
Sixth and Lyles Sts., Turkey
806-423-1491

Buddy Holly Statue/Walk of Fame
Between 7th and 8th Sts.
at Ave. Q, Lubbock

Gas Light
5212 57th St., Lubbock
806-785-1720

Buddy Holly Center
1801 Crickets Ave., Lubbock
806-775-3560
www.buddyhollycenter.org

Buddy Holly's Grave
City of Lubbock Cemetery
2100 E. 34th St., Lubbock

Lazy T B&B
On the fringes of Fredericksburg
866-244-7897
www.lazytbandb.com

Hondo's
312 W. Main St., Fredericksburg
830-997-1633
www.hondosonmain.com

Auslander Biergarten
323 E. Main St., Fredericksburg
830-997-7714
www.theauslander.com

Stonehenge II
FM 1340, near Hunt

Hangar Hotel
155 Airport Rd., Fredericksburg
830-997-9990
www.hangarhotel.com

Cathedral of Junk
4422 Lareina Dr., Austin
512-299-7413

Toy Joy
2900 Guadalupe St., Austin
512-320-0090
www.toyjoy.com

James A. Michener's Grave
Austin Memorial Park
2800 Hancock Dr., Austin

Ginny's Little Longhorn Saloon
5434 Burnet Rd., Austin
512-458-1813
www.ginnyslittlelonghorn.com

Longbranch Inn
1133 E. 11 St., Austin
512-472-5591
www.longbranchinn.com

Stevie Ray Vaughan Statue
South shore of Town Lake,
just west of S. First St., Austin

Daniel Johnston's
Jeremiah the Innocent **Mural**
2100 Guadalupe St., Austin

Museum of the Weird
412 E. 6th St., Austin, in the
back of Lucky Lizard Curios & Gifts
512-476-5493
www.museumoftheweird.com

Casino El Camino
517 E. Sixth St., Austin
512-469-9330
www.casinoelcamino.net

Mean Eyed Cat
1621 W. Fifth St., Austin
512-472-6326
www.themeaneyedcat.com

Lala's Little Nugget
2207 Justin Ln., Austin
512-453-2521

**Pots and Plants
Garden Center**
5902 Bee Caves Rd. (at Loop 360)
512-327-4564
www.plasticpinkflamingos.com

**Bob Bullock Texas State
History Museum**
1800 N. Congress Ave., Austin
512-936-4649
www.thestoryoftexas.com

**Spider House
Patio Bar & Cafe**
2908 Fruth St., Austin
512-480-9562
www.spiderhousecafe.com

Carousel Lounge
1110 E. 52nd, Austin
512-452-6790

Curra's Grill
614 E. Oltorf St., Austin
512-444-0012
www.currasgrill.com

G & S Lounge
2420 S. 1st St., Austin
512-707-8702

Antone's
213 W. Fifth St., Austin
512-320-8424
www.antones.net

Spoetzl Brewery
603 E. Brewery St., Shiner
361-594-4294
www.shiner.com

Gruene Hall
1281 Gruene Rd., New Braunfels
830-606-1281
www.gruenehall.com

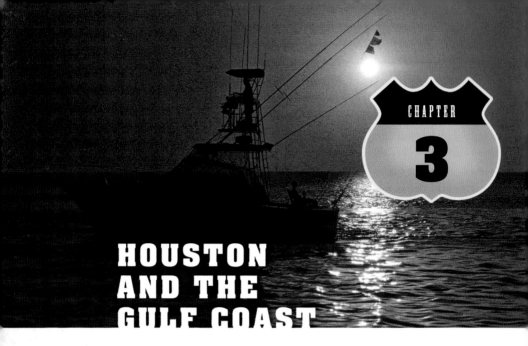

HOUSTON AND THE GULF COAST

INTRODUCTION

With a labyrinth of highways, humidity, and a funky personality, Houston is like the bastard child of New Orleans and Los Angeles, only without the voodoo or the movie stars. The impact of the lack of stars in Houston, however, is cushioned by the large population of people who are stars in their own minds, a condition usually evidenced by a jacked-up truck or a pair of fake tits. It's hard to miss either: the former fill up your entire rearview mirror and the latter are artfully displayed by their owners' plunging necklines.

This sprawling, sweaty city has virtually no zoning, so you'll find old neighborhoods interspersed with industry interspersed with more than a little quirk. There are oddball public art landmarks, fire-belching oil facilities, old buildings and new, and there is no reason or rhyme to the planning. In comparison with orderly, reserved Dallas, Houston is chaotic and ornery—and that's not necessarily a bad thing.

But Houston is only Houston because it is forty-five miles from Galveston. Only after a hurricane decimated Texas's then-commercial capital twice in 1900 did the inland city truly take root as the Lone Star State's foremost trade center. The discovery of oil in the region in the early twentieth century added considerable fuel to Houston's capitalist fire, which might have peaked a century later in August 2000, when Enron's stock price peaked at $90.

But boom and bust are part of the natural cycle in these parts. North and south of Galveston, hurricanes have shaped and reshaped the Texas Gulf Coast for eons and show no signs of letting up anytime soon. Because of this, you can get some great room rates if you travel here during the rainy season. The weather could be beautiful and storm free, just another week in paradise—or maybe you'll get to enjoy the authentic experience of evacuating paradise.

STATS & FACTS

- *Houston* was the first word ever spoken from the moon.

- With wind speeds topping 150 miles an hour, the Indianola Hurricane of 1886 is the most powerful hurricane to ever make landfall in Texas. It literally wiped Indianola off the map. The town, still reeling from an 1875 hurricane, was never rebuilt.

- The first Whataburger opened in Corpus Christi in 1950.

- The Aransas National Wildlife Refuge is the winter haven for the country's only flock of whooping cranes.

- The historic King Ranch in Kingsville is bigger than Rhode Island.

BIG THINGS AND OTHER ROAD ART

Orange Show Center for Visionary Art
2402 Munger St., Houston
713-926-6368
www.orangeshow.org

Jefferson Davis McKissack, the mastermind behind the Orange Show, has been quoted as saying, "You could take 100,000 architects and 100,000 engineers and all of them together couldn't conceive of a show like this." The late Houston postal worker's show is dedicated to the healthful effects of the orange, thus *The Orange Show*. A remarkably devoted champion of the fruit, McKissack spent twenty-five years building this ramshackle, Rube Goldbergian folk-art labyrinth, adorned with spinning wheels, concrete lions, and signs and tiled inscriptions like "Clown found happiness by drinking fresh cold orange juice every day" and "I love oranges." Other displays detail how oranges perfectly capture the sun's energy and convert it into something suitable for human consumption.

Read:
- The Big Rich: The Rise and Fall of the Greatest Texas Oil Fortunes by Bryan Burrough
- Isaac's Storm: A Man, a Time, and the Deadliest Hurricane in History by Erik Larson
- Snow White by Donald Barthelme

Listen:
- Lyle Lovett and His Large Band by Lyle Lovett
- Degüello by ZZ Top
- We Can't Be Stopped by Geto Boys
- "Midnight Special" by Leadbelly

Watch:
- Urban Cowboy
- Apollo 13
- Rushmore
- Enron: The Smartest Guys in the Room

To-Do Checklist:
- Make lots of money
- Go to Mission Control (and, if you have time, outer space)
- Take time to stop and smell the petrochemicals

McKissack started working on his show in 1955 and was able to populate it with all sorts of weird artifacts he found on his postal route in an era when downtown Houston was in serious decline. He put in bleacher seating, a cafeteria, and a gift shop. He devised customer satisfaction ballots that included the question, Do you say the Orange Show is the most beautiful show on Earth?

Ever the optimist, McKissack had extremely high hopes, says Orange Show spokesperson Stephen Bridges. "He thought it would be the biggest thing since the Astrodome. He loved to take people through here and he was very proud. But we still don't know what the show was." After 40,000 hours of labor, McKissack opened the place to the public in 1979 and 250 showed up on the first day, but the customers slowed to a trickle in just a few weeks. "He got depressed," says Bridges. Seven months after it opened, McKissack died, perhaps of a broken heart.

But local arts patrons saved McKissack's folk-art environment from demolition. It's since become the heart of Houston's distinctively eccentric arts scene. In a sense, the Orange Show has fulfilled its creator's quirky vision as one of the biggest—and oddest—shows in town.

ArtCar Museum
140 Heights Blvd., Houston
713-861-5526
www.artcarmuseum.com

Houston is without a doubt the center of the international art car phenomenon. The city's annual ArtCar Parade in May draws around a quarter-million people and 250 cars that look like bugs and dinosaurs and rats, cars from the future, and cars covered with fruit and mirrors and all sorts of other weird shit. If you can't make it here for the big event in May, the ArtCar Museum is one of the coolest free museums anywhere, any time of year. The so-called Garage Mahal focuses on vehicular masterworks and other disciplines well outside of the mainstream art world, with regularly rotating exhibits that always include at least five art cars on temporary loan, parked in the galleries.

Beer Can House
222 Malone St., Houston
www.beercanhouse.org

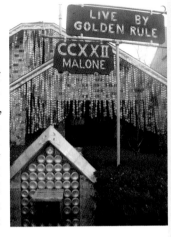

Born in 1912, John Milkovisch came of age during the Great Depression, and the experience made him a very thrifty man, albeit one with a big smile and an even bigger beer gut. He saved every can from every beer he ever drank, fastidiously cutting off the top and the bottom and unrolling the aluminum flat. He stored them until he was struck with inspiration in 1968 to begin covering his house with them. His wife, Mary, did not mind.

After he retired from his job with the railroad in 1976, he worked at it pretty much full time until the entire house was clad in flattened beer cans. Milkovisch also made garlands from the tops and bottoms of said cans that chatter softly in the wind, and he drilled holes in the fence and filled them with marbles. Milkovisch's twelve-ounce-at-a-time aluminum siding saved the Milkovischs money on their air-conditioning bills. You'll see all kinds of brands here—Falstaff, Busch, Buckhorn, Texas Pride, even a few plain old Budweisers. Seems Milkovisch drank whatever was cheapest. He passed away in 1988, and his ashes were spread on the property he worked so hard and drank so much beer to create.

The Flower Man
2305 Francis St., Houston

Cleveland "The Flower Man" Turner was a wayward, skid-row bum who prayed not to be a drunk and promised God a garden in return. When he finally got sober, he indeed planted what one could loosely describe as a garden. In his yard at his place in Houston's poor Third Ward, Cleveland's garden includes everything from a plastic Santa, a Cabbage Patch Kid, plastic camels, real plants, fake plants, shards of pottery, a broken-down art car, you name it. The garden even extends inside Cleveland's house—he is constantly creating a masterpiece in the eye of one beholder or another out of discarded toys, trash, and treasure.

Huge Spotted Hydrant
Walnut and Mulberry Sts., Beaumont
409-880-3927
www.firemuseumoftexas.org

Outside the Fire Museum of Texas stands a white twenty-four-foot fire hydrant with black spots, which was proudly dedicated in 1999 as the world's largest fire hydrant. The two-ton statue, originally created to promote Disney's live-action *101 Dalmatians* and now surrounded by regular-sized spotted hydrants on the sidewalk, has since been outdone by hydrants in South Carolina and Manitoba, but it's still plenty big.

Forbidden Gardens
23500 Franz Rd., Katy
281-347-8000
www.forbidden-gardens.com

Real-estate tycoon Ira Poon funded the 1990s construction of this attraction just west of Houston as a testament to Chinese history. The sprawling property features a one-third scale model of one of the greatest archaeological finds ever—Emperor Qin's ancient tomb and its resident army of 6,000 terra-cotta soldiers who protect his body—and an elaborate model of the Forbidden City. It is a monumental work of Chinese-influenced roadside Americana, sure, but the soldiers here have not weathered the hot and humid climate very well. Poon is said to do very little promotion so he can have the place to himself.

R.I.P.

Sam Houston, 1793–1863
Oakwood Cemetery
9th St. and Ave. I, Huntsville

An often controversial icon of Texas history, Sam Houston moved from Tennessee to Tejas in 1832 and four years later led the state to independence with a military victory over Santa Anna at the Battle of San Jacinto. He served as president of the Republic of Texas, then as a United States senator after Texas statehood, and in 1859 began his term as governor of Texas. Although he was a slave owner, he opposed secession from the United States but was forced out by the pro-secession majority, ending his career at the beginning of the Civil War. He died in Huntsville. His gravesite has a sixty-seven-foot statue of his likeness that would be the tallest sculpture in Texas if it weren't for that superfluous blade of grass topping the tongue of the giraffe at the Dallas Zoo.

Howard Hughes, 1905–1976
Glenwood Cemetery
2525 Washington Ave., Houston
713-864-7886
www.glenwoodcemetery.org

Howard Robard Hughes Jr. inherited his family's oil-drilling-bit fortune at the age of nineteen and went on to direct and produce films in Hollywood; date starlets; design, build, and pilot flying machines of all manner; and battle obsessive-compulsive tendencies to stack and restack tissue boxes and pee in jars. He grew the $1 million inheritance into a $2 billion fortune over the years and was arguably the world's richest man for a spell in the 1960s. In the last decade of his life, he bounced from penthouse to penthouse, gobbling Baskin-Robbins banana-nut ice cream, then French vanilla ice cream, and only cutting his hair and nails once a year. He died either in his private plane or an Acapulco penthouse, depending on who is telling the story, weighing a mere ninety pounds, without a valid will.

1900 Hurricane Memorial
48th St. and Seawall Blvd., Galveston

Still the most devastating natural disaster in US history, the category-four hurricane that slammed into Galveston Island on September 9, 1900, killing an estimated 8,000 people, is memorialized in bronze by local artist David Moore. Local forecasters believed the storm would steer north up the Atlantic coast, leading few people to evacuate before it struck. One in five

Galveston residents lost their lives in the storm or the subsequent flooding, and 30,000 islanders—or nearly everyone else—lost their homes. Galveston never quite recovered its luster as one of Texas's most preeminent cities, as Houston became the state's population center and commercial hub. As Hurricane Ike reminded the world in 2008, Galveston still has a precarious front-row seat for each and every hurricane season. Ike tried his best to blow down the 1900 memorial, but the sculpture survived without as much as a scratch.

Selena, 1971–1995
Memorial, Shoreline Blvd.
at People's St.,
Corpus Christi Grave,
Seaside Memorial Park,
5347 Ocean Dr., Corpus Christi

The Mexican Madonna, Selena was a rising Tejano star who outdrew superstars like George Strait and Reba McEntire when she played the Astrodome months before her death. Shot in the back by the president of her fan club, she bled to death in the lobby of a Days Inn before she turned twenty-four. Her star still burns bright in her hometown of Corpus Christi—fans regularly travel from afar to pay their respects at her memorial on Corpus Christi Bay.

National Museum of Funeral History
415 Barren Springs Dr., Houston
281-876-3063
www.nmfh.org

If you're into coffins, hearses, and the history of American embalming, this is the museum for you. The collection features the Money Casket (perfect for the greediest dead people);

an exhibit covering "The Funerals of the Famous," with pro-
grams and mementos from the burials of Elvis, John Gotti,
Rodney Dangerfield, and King Edward VII; Ghanian coffins
shaped like crabs and eagles; and much more. An embalming
room depicts how it was done on the Civil War battlefield
by Dr. Thomas Holmes, The Father of American Embalming,
and a replica of an old-school casket factory offers a behind-
the-scenes look at historic coffin making. The gift shop can
fill any funeral-related gift need you might have, from the
best-selling T-shirts bearing the slogan Every Day Above
Ground is a Good One, to coffin-shaped paperweights and
putters to caskets designed specifically for bottles of wine.

VICE

Houston Nightlife

Serving wine and beer and accepting cash only, La Carafe
(813 Congress St., 713-229-9399) is the perfect downtown
dive. It's located in an allegedly haunted 1847 building, featuring huge globes of wax behind the bar from decades of
candles dripping, walls covered in all manner of pictures and

paintings, and the off-kilter bar itself, carved with so many initials it is no longer flat. In Midtown, Leon's Lounge (1006 Mcgowen St., 713-659-3052) is another retro dive. The joint's been open since 1947 and offers an ambiance that effortlessly meshes the smell of stale beer, fancy chandeliers, and a killer jukebox. The Continental Club (3700 Main St., 713-529-9899, www.continentalclub.com) is the larger-but-younger cousin of Austin's legendary club. Opened in a former grocery store in 2000, this joint lives up to its hallowed name. In Montrose, the bare-bones, open-air West Alabama Ice House (1919 W. Alabama St., 713-528-6874) is the ultimate neighborhood bar, serving beer nightly and hot dogs on Fridays, and offering a

diversion in the form of a basketball hoop out back. If it's cheap beer you're after, Valhalla (6100 Main St., 713-348-3258, http:// Valhalla.rice.edu) is a nonprofit beer hall on campus for Rice University grad students. A twelve-ounce cup of Shiner Bock will set you back all of $1. On the weird end of the spectrum is Notsuoh (314 Main St., 713-409-4750), decorated with mannequins and bicycles and birdcages. And you have to knock twice to get into the long-standing offbeat Tex-Mex joint and hippie haven that is the Last Concert Cafe (1403 Nance St., 713-226-8563, www.lastconcert.com).

Mardi Gras in Galveston
www.mardigrasgalveston.com

Like many of its Gulf Coast brethren, Galveston throws one hell of a Mardi Gras party every Fat Tuesday, complete with parades, costumes, beads, boobs, and all hell breaking loose. The city started celebrating Mardi Gras in the 1800s, but the public festivities died off during World War II. The 1980s saw the party rise again, and it now attracts some 250,000 revelers each year.

Poop Deck
2928 Seawall Blvd., Galveston
409-763-9151

An eccentric but welcoming ambiance of maritime kitsch, a fridge plastered with Polaroids of females flashing their breasts, and a deck overlooking the Gulf of Mexico (thankfully free of poop), the Poop Deck does not disappoint. Served by bartenders wearing shipmate-style uniforms with Daisy

Dukes, regulars drink and drawl as they watch the surfers paddle out and the hurricanes roll in—this place famously does not shut down for the latter.

Dixie Chicken
307 University Dr.,
Bryan-College Station
979-846-2322
www.dixiechicken.com

Carousing in Bryan-College Station doesn't get any louder or more colorful than this ramshackle Texas A&M hangout. The proprietors say the bar serves more beer per square foot than any other watering hole in the country, and I don't doubt the claim. The offerings: cold beer, greasy grub, live music, pool tables, and, of course, live rattlesnakes behind panes of glass.

Executive Surf Club
309 N. Water St.,
Corpus Christi
361-884-7873
www.executivesurfclub.com

A diverse crowd eats and drinks at this joint in the Water Street Market, featuring an immense fishing lure above the bar, swimming trunks on the men's room door, and live music on most nights. With thirty beers on draft and a great happy hour, this is just the place to soothe that sunburn with two or four cold ones and a shrimp po'boy.

Texas Prison Museum
491 TX Hwy. 75 N., Huntsville
936-295-2155
www.txprisonmuseum.org

About 150,000 Texans are in prison—more than 400 of them on death row—and the state's prison industry is a $2.5 billion business. You'll learn all of that, plus how to make a shank out of a fork, at the Texas Prison Museum in the state's most prison-heavy city, Huntsville. (Ask for the free prison driving-tour map.) Exhibits include a model cell with a bunk, a Bible, and a toilet (for Display Purposes Only, according to a sign), prisoners' arts and crafts projects, a display covering Texas legends Bonnie and Clyde, a case full of confiscated contraband (shanks, shivs, stills, drug paraphernalia, and escape tools), and several covering the death penalty in Texas. The retired electric chair known as "Old Sparky" is here, the state's means of execution from 1924 to 1964. There are also placards covering specific executions, last meals, and quotes from prisoners before their execution and members of the victims' families afterward. According to one of the latter, "There is no such thing as closure."

STAR MAPS

- Janis Joplin was born and raised in Port Arthur, on the far eastern fringe of the Texas Gulf Coast. The Museum of the Gulf Coast (700 Procter St., 409-982-7000, www.museumofthegulfcoast.org) has a number of the legendary psychedelic rock siren's personal effects and a replica of her rainbow-painted Porsche. Fans can get a brochure at the museum or local chamber of commerce (800-235-7822, www  .portarthurtexas. com) with a fifteen- stop driving tour, which includes the hospital where Joplin was born, her former homes and schools, and even her baptismal church.

- The schools attended by Jason Schwartzman's character Max in *Rushmore*, directed by Houston native Wes Anderson, are Lamar High School and St. John's on Westheimer Road at River Oaks Boulevard.

- The silicon breast implant was invented in Houston by plastic surgeons Thomas Cronin and Frank Gerow in 1961, altering Hollywood's topography and half of the country's body image forever.

- The late Anna Nicole Smith met elderly oil tycoon J. Howard Marshall when she was dancing at Gigi's Cabaret (11150 Northwest Freeway, 713-686-3401) in 1991. After she became the 1993 Playmate of the Year, they married in 1994, when she was twenty-six and he was eighty-nine. He died fourteen months later, setting off a bizarre inheritance battle. Gigi's is now one of the worst strip clubs in Texas.

HUH?

The Health Museum's Amazing Body Pavilion
1515 Hermann Dr., Houston
713-521-1515
www.thehealthmuseum.org

If you've ever wanted to delve right into a human body without getting too dirty in the process, this is the place. From the face to the heart to the guts, you get a close-up view on such exhibits as a 27.5-foot intestine and clogged artery replicas. Some of the displays are fittingly bizarre, especially the immense walk-through brain and its somewhat psychedelic depiction of the biomechanics of thought.

Huge Presidents' Heads and Big Beatles
SculpturWorx
2500 Summer St., Houston

David Adickes likes to work big. His Sam Houston statue in Huntsville is second-biggest in Texas by a technicality in the

form of a metal blade of grass atop the tongue of the giraffe at the Dallas Zoo. His studio in Houston has a yard of immense presidents' heads, and not just the Rushmore stars—Andrew Johnson, George H. W. Bush, Grover Cleveland, and others are outside his studio and eminently photographable until their ultimate relocation elsewhere. Playing backup to these humongous presidential heads is a thirty-six-foot Fab Four. The big Beatles are apparently permanent fixtures at Adickes's place in the Heights, but the presidential busts are awaiting installation in various presidential-themed projects around the country. Adickes welcomes people to check out his work, so don't be shy wandering the yard with your digital camera.

Houston Tunnels

Tours available from The Tunnel Lady
713-222-9255
www.houston-tunnels.com

There are roughly seven miles of tunnels twenty feet below downtown Houston, full of Starbucks, barbershops, dentists, delis, gift shops, and other businesses. These urban caverns date back to the 1920s, during one boom time, and were expanded during another building boom downtown in the 1970s and 1980s. Most access points are inside buildings above the tunnels, while Wells Fargo Plaza (1000 Louisiana St.) has access from the street. During the sweltering summer months, downtown Houston can be a ghost town on the surface, only to be bustling in its air-conditioned underbelly.

GRUB

Houston: The Eating-Out Capital of the USA

Houstonians eat out more than residents of any other major American city, and they have 8,000 restaurants to choose from. Not only is there a remarkably deep well of eateries here, but the prices are among the lowest in the country.

A meal in Houston is usually about half the price of one in New York City.

Some locals say the traffic is so bad, you don't have time to cook. Others say it's so hot, you don't even want to turn on the oven. Others still just think it's simply a result of the free market prevailing over hunger—in a very big way.

So name your cuisine, be it barbecue, French, Thai, seafood, Mexican, Cajun, Italian, New American, or greasy burgers. Houston has it all, and then some. A few picks of the 8,000 possibilities:

Burgers: Lankford Grocery & Market (88 Dennis St., 713-522-9555) is no longer a store but a standout for massive, old-fashioned cheeseburgers, onion rings, and other fried and grilled delicacies.

Barbecue: Goode Co. Texas Bar-B-Q (5109 Kirby Dr., 713-522-2530, www.goodecompany.com) offers cheap beef brisket, killer jalapeño cheese bread, and more Texas kitsch on the wall than you can categorize in one meal.

Vietnamese: Les Givral's Kahve (2704 Milam, 713-529-1736, www.lesgivrals.com) specializes in Vietnamese sandwiches, pho, and rice dishes—and nothing is more than $8.

Mexican: Irma's (22 N. Chenevert St., 713-222-0767) is a dinky spot by the ballpark downtown serving incomparable home-cooked Mexican breakfasts and lunches and sensational fresh-fruit lemonade.

Thai: Kanomwan (736 1/2 Telephone Rd., 713-923-4236) might not look like much, but it tastes like unholy rapture—in a good way.

Gulf Coast Seafood

Dead spot south of Louisiana notwithstanding, the Gulf of Mexico is a remarkably biodiverse body of water, alive with sharks, sea turtles, and dolphins, as well as plenty of good animals to eat. Beer-battered shrimp, barbecued crab, and fried flounder are among the most signature dishes of the Third Coast. Near the Louisiana state line you'll also find some blackened-fish dishes, kingfish creole, and seafood gumbo. Closer to Mexico, ceviche and fish tacos appear on the menus.

There are many great shrimp shacks and oyster bars up and down the Texas Gulf Coast, including Esther's Seafood & Oyster Bar (7327 Rainbow Ln. in Port Arthur, 409-962-6268, www.estherscajunseafood.com), Snoopy's Pier under the JFK causeway in Corpus Christi (13313 S. Padre Island Dr., 361-949-8815) and Lost Galleon (102 E. Queen Isabella Blvd., Port Isabel, 956-943-4400).

SLEEPS

Tarpon Inn
200 E. Cotter Ave., Port Aransas
361-749-5555
www.thetarponinn.com

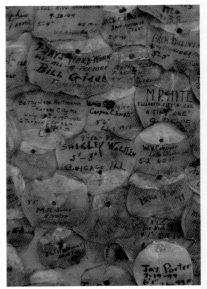

Opened in 1886—and destroyed by fire and hurricane in the time since—the Tarpon Inn is Port Aransas's original lodging, named for the fish formerly most likely to be caught during a visitor's stay. Back in the day, successful anglers—including FDR, Duncan Hines, and Hedy Lamarr—would sign a tarpon scale and tack it to the lobby wall, thus the lobby wall was covered from floor to ceiling in dried fish scales. However, tarpon are rarely caught around Port Aransas today, so don't count on adding one. Fronted by a shady front porch, the hurricane-proof building is an engineering marvel, with perfectly aligned pilings extending from the attic into the earth.

Tee Pee Motel

4098 E. Business 59, Wharton
979-282-TIPI
www.teepeemotel.net

Built in 1942 as part of a national chain of tee pee motels, Wharton's Tee Pee Motel offers up ten individual stucco teepees that sheath rooms fairly typical of what you'd expect in a roadside motel. After the place was abandoned to the elements in the 1980s, new owners restored the kitschy hostelry in 2005, and once again opened the fake teepees to overnight guests.

Von Minden Hotel

607 Lyons Ave., Schulenburg
512-203-6720
www.myspace.com/vonmindenhotel

Built in the late 1920s and only changing hands once in the subsequent eight decades, the Von Minden Hotel is the most notoriously haunted hotel in the Lone Star State. A railroad worker who died in room twenty-three, a suicidal World War II vet who jumped from room thirty-seven, and the enigmatically named Ms. X just can't seem to leave the property behind. Beyond the paranormal activity, also on the property are a pizzeria and the historic Cozy Theatre, part of the hotel since it opened and still playing movies to this day.

MISC.

Padre Island National Seashore

Southeast of Corpus Christi
361-949-8068
www.nps.gov/pais

Just a few thousand years old, this spindly seventy-mile ribbon of beach and dunes and life is the longest undeveloped stretch of barrier island on the planet, slowly but surely expanding toward the Texas mainland as the elements carry sand west. In all, Padre Island is 130 miles long and less than a mile wide, making it the world's longest barrier island and the second largest island in the continental United States after New York's Long Island.

One of only six hypersaline lagoons on the planet, Laguna Madre is between Padre Island and the mainland, in places as much as three times saltier than the ocean. The lagoon, the island, and the Gulf of Mexico offer three radically different ecosystems. The endangered Kemp's ridley sea turtle nests here. Volunteers collect the eggs to nurture them until they hatch, since predators and tides often took out the eggs on land—just as shrimpers' nets have taken out turtles in the Gulf of Mexico. In recent years, wildlife officials have released more than 10,000 hatchlings.

With a good four-wheel drive, you can drive the entire length of the national seashore and find a solid stretch of paradise to have to yourself. Solitude—check. Suntan lotion, swimming suits, and sleeping bags—check. A fully stocked cooler—check. Your camp at the water's edge is yours to fish, beachcomb, or swim—or just dawdle the day away with the seashells, sand castles, and shorebirds.

Big Thicket National Preserve
North of Beaumont
409-951-6725
www.nps.gov/bith

A confluence of ecosystems—swamp, forest, plains, and desert—Big Thicket is as wild and dense a wilderness as you'll find anywhere. Thousands of plant species (including four out of five insect-eating varieties in North America) provide cover for everything from alligators to bluebirds. The preserve, just under 100,000 acres, is the last chunk of a massive backwoods slowly carved away by the sawmills, the railroads, and the oil fields.

OIL, POWER, AND MONEY

5 DAYS, 300 MILES

"One hundred and forty million went into the property," says the desk clerk to the gray-haired couple in front of me. I'm waiting to check in at the La Torretta Del Lago Resort & Spa in Montgomery, Texas, on the shores of Lake Conroe, an hour north of Houston. "That's a lot of money."

"That is a lot of money," chuckles the man.

But is it? What exactly passes for "a lot of money" these days? It seems $140 million is just a drop in the bucket, and that bucket has a gaping hole in the bottom of it.

It's a drab and gray afternoon. From my balcony on the seventeenth floor, I can see the fountain at the entrance, a water park with slides and a massive bucket that fills and overturns on the empty pool every minute or so, a golf course, tennis courts, lakefront luxury homes, and a couple of boats cruising the lake. The hotel is almost empty—a trio of conferences departed earlier in the day.

Stuart, who works for the PR firm that represents the resort, calls a few minutes later and apologizes for the weather. "Not a problem," I respond. "Whatcha gonna do?"

We meet an hour later in the lobby. He tells me the resort had been neglected by the former owners, but the new owners injected $140 million into the place. There's a sushi bar, a piano bar, a nightclub, racquetball courts, and collectible chess sets under glass in the lobby.

He takes me out to the beautiful but cold and dark pool area. "There's also a sandy beach over there," Stuart adds, pointing into the inky blackness. "There will be a 300-slip marina with a market. Everything you could imagine."

A loud splash interrupts his spiel, as the big bucket dumps its load in the pool about 100 yards away. "I think that's 300 gallons," Stuart remarks.

We take a van tour with a driver and a security guy. My eyes glaze over. I can't even feign interest. At times, I feel an alien is going to burst from the crown of my skull.

I've toured well over 1,000 hotels and B&Bs and resorts and motels over the course of my travel-writing career. Many of them comp me a room for my troubles, an implicit and admittedly somewhat corrupt deal in which the lodging hopes their generosity translates to ink. I make no guarantees, but am more than willing to take a free room. I need a place to type and sleep and figure the room would be going unused.

I doubt I will generate much publicity for this particular resort. Does that make me more or less corrupt?

Stuart buys me dinner, another borderline corrupt travel-writer perk, and I shamelessly down a bowl of seafood chowder, a terrific salmon dish, and three Shiner Bocks. He loosens up after selling me on the finer points of the resort and gets enthusiastic talking about Houston's renaissance and its varied neighborhoods, dubbing River Oaks "the Beverly Hills of Houston."

We talk about Houston's Enron fiasco of 2001. "I had a friend who worked there who could not tell you what he did," Stuart says. We also discuss the impact of low oil prices on Houston and the term *economic crisis*. "It's gotten to be a media buzzword," I insist. "How long can a crisis go on? I thought a crisis was like a house on fire—something must be done *now*!"

It seems that there is simply not enough money out there. Maybe it's tied up in places like this, illiquid in waterslides and custom carpeting, glass towers and Israeli interior design.

Some seem to think we can buy ourselves out of our problems by spending more money. Maybe that's true. But money can't buy happiness. Or the weather.

I bid Stuart goodnight and the elevator rockets me back up to the seventeenth floor.

· · · · ·

After a good night's sleep, I get a call from Kyra, the hotel's internal marketing person, who asks if I want to go through with the scheduled boat tour. "The weather is a little inclement," she says.

Navigating the halls, surprisingly alive with the sounds of power tools, I meet her in the lobby and decide to go through with it. With a nice smile and mascara-saturated eyelashes, she looks a little taken aback, but is a good sport. We meet Greg, the resort's licensed captain, at the marina and head out across the foggy lake in a brand-new motorboat.

Greg tells me of the lake's creation in 1979 as a tertiary water supply for Houston. He points to the highly rated Walden Peninsula Golf Course on the left. We cruise under power lines into the heart of the lake, and he says that Hurricane Ike tore through the area four months before with winds blowing at 110 miles an hour. "There was substantial damage to the lake," he says. "It was rough."

Greg points out all sorts of new developments and touts the local real-estate market as gravity defying. "Waterfront property here has gone absolutely crazy," he says—$750,000 gets you 100 or so feet of frontage. He says it's defied the national housing trend, as have many things in the Houston area. "Like everything else, it's going up. They're not selling as many, but it's not going down." There is massive commercial development in the area, including the new marina, which is neighbored by huge piles of freshly moved earth on the shore.

On the way back, Greg says the lake's Bentwater development has some serious mansions. "Dick Cheney's got a house there, Hakeem Olajuwon, Roger Clemens," he says. Hopefully, Hakeem has the good sense to not associate with Roger and Dick.

He tells me sailing is big on the lake and invites me back in the summer to go out on his personal sailboat, then decries the day's weather. "It's going to be 70 degrees tomorrow. Go figure."

Two hours later, I'm getting off Interstate 45 South at the Houston Space Center exit. Parking at the visitors lot, I finagle my press ticket for the Level Nine Tour, named for the top floor of the highest building at the Johnson Space Center. Soon I'm on a bus with nine tourists paying the full $85 price for the five-hour tour, along with two Japanese journalists, an international tourism marketer for the Houston visitors bureau, and our guide, David, a retired NASA operations guy who worked at the agency as an engineer starting in 1968, a year before Neil Armstrong took his first step on the moon.

On the way to the employee cafeteria for lunch, the van passes Texas longhorns grazing on NASA property. Tang and freeze-dried ice cream are, of course, available, but I go for a chicken wrap and iced tea instead.

Eating, I absentmindedly read the visitors guide, which mentions space exploration as human destiny. Is it also human destiny to wreck Planet Earth in pursuit of money? And if so, will the rich move to the moon once our planet is uninhabitable?

The tourism rep and the two Japanese journalists join me at my table. The rep, a Colombian in her twenties, tells me she promotes Houston to Latin America, Asia, and the Middle East. The journalists work for the magazine that goes out to Japanese Visa Gold cardholders.

After lunch, we get back in the van and continue on the tour. David points out the building where astronauts are quarantined for three to five days before liftoff to avoid catching a cold. He tells us that Rice University owns the

campus and leases it back to NASA for only $1 a year, and that the Johnson Space Center is one of ten NASA units responsible for mission control and training.

"I want you to know where we've been, where we're going, and why we're going there," David adds.

Our first stop is the Sonny Carter Training Facility, the home of the Neutral Buoyancy Laboratory, which is basically a massive indoor pool where astronauts train underwater on scale mockups of the *International Space Station*, the Hubble Telescope, and a space shuttle to prepare for upcoming missions. Assisted by teams of safety divers, the astronauts are in their full flight suits, weighted down for neutral buoyancy—you don't float or sink—and they rehearse the various maneuvers and technical projects they'll need to do later on a space walk.

"Space walks last up to seven hours, and thus astronauts wear diapers," David notes. "Every astronaut uses it, I guarantee you," he adds. "They're trained to use it." I'd like to see that reverse potty-training class.

On the drive to the main NASA campus, David covers *Sputnik*, the world's first satellite, Ham, the American chimpanzee astronaut, and Laika, the Russian cosmonaut dog. He also touches on the next twenty years for NASA: "2020, we'll have boots back on the moon. 2030, we'll be on Mars."

Out first stop is the observation room behind Space Shuttle Mission Control (in a qualifications session, not a real mission), then International Space Station Mission Control (which operates 24/7, 365 days a year), and finally Mission Control 1, the national historic landmark where all the famous Apollo missions

"Houston, we have a tourist!"

were tethered to Houston for support—the moon landing and the infamous, and nearly disastrous, Apollo 13.

"'Houston, Tranquility Base here,'" says David. "'The *Eagle* has landed.' Six hundred million people, one-fifth of the world's population, heard it on this speaker. 'Houston, we have a problem,' came through this speaker."

He also tells us that NASA secretaries bought the flag that Neil Armstrong and Buzz Aldrin planted on the moon at Sears for $5 during their lunch break. And apparently the United Nations was not too keen on the flag-planting at the time. But what good is power in a peaceful world?

Our final stop is the rocket yard, where we see the monstrous *Saturn V* that carried the Apollo missions out of the atmosphere. David says that the thing burned fifteen tons a second immediately after liftoff in the process of generating 7.5 million pounds of thrust—just enough to carry a trio of astronauts out of the atmosphere.

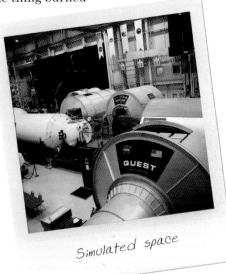

Simulated space

Walking around the huge rocket, I note the quotes on the wall from astronauts Alan Shepard—"When I looked back at the Earth, standing on the Moon, I cried."—and Gus Grissom—"The conquest of space is worth the risk of life." Grissom died in a fire during Apollo 1 training.

I think how the moon landing took place in the midst of the Vietnam War and the Cold War—it *was* part of the Cold War, in fact.

I'm almost on my way out when I decide to take a quick spin around the Starship Gallery in the main visitor center. I see an interactive quiz and take a wild stab answering a question, guessing Helium-3 is found on the moon. The computer informs me I'm correct, and that a space shuttle

full of this helium isotope would power the United States for a year without any radioactive by-product.

A wall-sized chalkboard lays it out even more succinctly in the next room. Intended for children, pictures depict a future space colony with farms and a mineral-extraction industry. "Shortages of fossil fuels on Earth will force human kind to develop new sources of energy in the twenty-first century." Fifty lunar harvesters could mine a ton of the stuff in a year, good enough for a year's worth of electricity for the entire country.

This must be the vision of the next conquest for ExxonMobil, Chevron, Shell, BP, and the rest: colonies of ultrabored, drugged-out drones running a Helium-3 mining and refining operation on the moon.

If 50 harvesters could support the United States, what could *5,000* harvesters support? And if there is no moon, what happens to the tides?

Such thoughts cycle through my gray matter on the rush-hour drive to The Magnolia Hotel downtown. My room was arranged by the aforementioned Houston tourism bureau. After checking in, I meet Lindsey, the bureau's director of domestic marketing and public relations, and we head to Reef, a swank restaurant in midtown. It is packed for a Monday night.

"People eat out here more than any other city," she tells me. She also tells me how Houston natives always come back home. "It's like the biggest little city—everybody knows everybody."

Biscuits with jalapeño jelly show up at our table, as well as a Shiner Bock for me and a glass of pinot noir for Lindsey.

She tells me of the seven miles of tunnels below downtown, essentially an underground mall, and The Tunnel Lady, who gives tours of them. "There are two aboveground Starbucks downtown," she notes.

How many are below ground? "Too many to count."

We order crab shooters and steamed mussels and seafood dinners.

When oil hit $140 a barrel in mid-2008, Houston's oil companies were throwing money at their employees, Lindsey tells me. "I don't know much about economics and supply and demand, but how did it go up and down like that? It's crazy."

She tells me Joanne Herring, the Houston socialite and conservative activist portrayed by Julia Roberts in *Charlie Wilson's War*, is still a fixture in Houston society, as are George H. W. and Barbara Bush. "They're everywhere, especially Astros games."

"There's a lot of power here," I say.

"There's a lot of money," Lindsey retorts.

"And it comes from oil, right?"

"Absolutely."

We split a lime tart for dessert.

She drops me off at the hotel. I wander out into the humid night and dodge one panhandler. A second one decides he'll accompany me to the bar.

"Just loan me a couple of dollars, man."

I protest that I don't have any ones.

"Give me a five."

I don't have a five.

"Get some change. C'mon, man. A couple of dollars."

I try to shake him but end

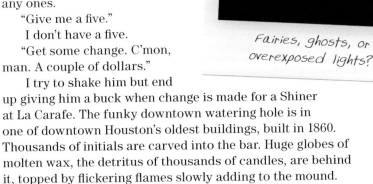

Fairies, ghosts, or overexposed lights?

up giving him a buck when change is made for a Shiner at La Carafe. The funky downtown watering hole is in one of downtown Houston's oldest buildings, built in 1860. Thousands of initials are carved into the bar. Huge globes of molten wax, the detritus of thousands of candles, are behind it, topped by flickering flames slowly adding to the mound.

The place is nearly empty. After the panhandler and three other customers leave, it's just the bartender, Patrick,

and me. We start talking about this and that, and he tells me about running into disgraced Enron CEO Jeff Skilling at a Houston hot-dog joint after his conviction in 2006. Apparently, Skilling was getting ready to dig in to a couple of chili dogs when the Bobby Fuller Four classic "I Fought the Law" came on the restaurant's sound system.

"I pull out my camera phone," says Patrick, "and he's like, 'Don't take my fucking picture!'"

"You must have been like, 'This is the most ironic moment—*ever*!'" I laugh.

After we discuss the possibility that Ken Lay faked his own death, Patrick tells me how Skilling and other Enron execs rode high-end motocross bikes around town and were total jerk-offs in many other respects—besides their record-setting financial fraud.

On the topic of oil and power, Patrick also advises I drive out to Pasadena—"Stinkadena"—before I split town, in order to see the city's acutely industrial petrochemical zone. "Flying in at night, it looks like something out of *Blade Runner*," he tells me. Patrick also tells me that he plays drums for a local band, Umbrella Man, and invites me to a gig the next night at the Continental Club.

Another panhandler hits me up for change on my walk back to The Magnolia. There are few things in this world that will possess men to either beg on the street from strangers or ride motocross to prove their manliness as they scale the corporate ladder.

· · · · ·

Tuesday is a busy day. I write for an hour before heading to the Orange Show for a tour of Houston's folk art with Stephen, the Orange Show Center for Visionary Art's public-relations guy. After touring, we stop at the Beer Can House and a store called Wabash Feed, where chickens and rabbits are available alongside beer, produce, and garden art.

Then we move on to Howard Hughes's grave, then an industrial yard populated by gargantuan sculptures of

Purity never seemed
so impure

presidential heads. After lunch at the Lankford Grocery, we pay a visit to The Flower Man. I'm impressed by just how distinctly odd Houston is.

Following my whirlwind tour with Stephen, I make another stop before returning downtown for the night. The Blaffer Gallery on the campus of the University of Houston has a temporary exhibit called *Texas Oil: Landscape of an Industry by The Center for Land Use Interpretation.*

The introductory passage on the wall discusses oil in general and Texas's oil business in focus. Pipelines make up "a circulatory system of the American land, moving the lifeblood of the economy."

"If the oil industry has a heart, then it is Texas," it concludes. "And Houston is its aorta."

There are two galleries, one with pictures of the Houston headquarters and offices of numerous major oil and energy companies, and another with pictures of major oil fields and petrochemical facilities in Houston and on the Gulf Coast. There are maps of the spider's web of pipelines in Texas, Alaska, and the greater United States. In the center of the second gallery, there is a transparent forty-two-gallon barrel of oil.

Another passage on the wall catches my eye: "In many ways, the industry is like the space program,

Plastic arms
strive moonward

but it is larger in scale, more ubiquitous, and terrestrial. It focuses on inner space: the opaque interior of the planet, a place alien to most of us."

What a strange and risky business, fraught with the perils of failing to strike oil, hurricanes, and extreme price volatility. It's also a beast that's grappling us all with its many tentacles, excreting money in Houston.

After making it back to The Magnolia, I take a walk around downtown, alive with commuters heading home after a day's work. It is a forest of mirrored skyscrapers housing mainly banks, law firms, and energy companies. There's Pennzoil Place, One Shell Plaza, Total Place.

The architecture in the sky and the people on the streets are both diverse lots. The only pattern is there is no pattern. Historic towers stand next to contemporary skyscrapers, a melting pot of people on the sidewalks below.

I see a crew replacing a mirrored window panel on a building by hoisting it 100 feet up. Three Asian waiters gamble at a table in Benihana, waiting for the dinner rush. A female security guard rouses a drunk from her nap on a corner.

My destination is 1400 Smith Street, the former Enron building. Many of the windows are boarded up, victims of Hurricane Ike. A striking $200 million, fifty-five-story tower, it's the largest empty office building in the United States and a highly visible monument to everything that's wrong with capitalism.

Just around the corner is KBR Tower, the home of the defense contractor and engineering firm. Enron might be gone, but business is still good for KBR, with contracts in Iraq and Afghanistan, and energy and construction projects all over the world.

At the Flying Saucer, the bar stools are filled with the after-work crowd's butts. I find an empty one for my own ass and order a beer from a dimpled bartendress. She delivers me a beer and my change. I notice the top single has the name Carlos and a local phone number scrawled above the serial number. I throw a different one in the tip jar and flip over Carlos's bill.

It's the pyramid with the floating eye that freaks me out. And does anybody even know what *Novus ordo seclorum* means? Or *Annuit Cœptis*? Why in the hell is this stuff on our money?

I hastily finish my beer and hit the complimentary happy hour at the hotel bar, striking up conversations with a couple of guys from Louisiana in town on oil business and another guy from Edinburg, Scotland, in town on wind business.

On the way to Continental Club in Midtown, I grab a sandwich and watch the guy in line behind me practice his golf swing as he waits for his order. Then I decide to call Carlos's number from the dollar to ask him what he thinks the eye floating over the pyramid means. He doesn't speak English.

At the club's bar a few minutes later, Patrick from La Carafe greets me and asks me how my day went. We talk about Howard Hughes's death (Patrick tells me he died on a flight), Dallas's condescension toward Houston, and the fact that his band Umbrella Man is not actually named after an alleged CIA operative who utilized an umbrella to either shoot poison darts or signal the shooters during JFK's assassination.

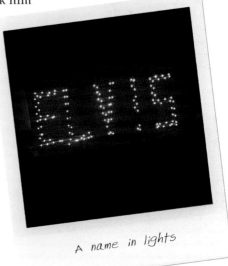

A name in lights

Hit-or-miss stand-up comedy precedes Umbrella Man, who offer a definitively Houston blend of Tejano, jazz, zydeco, and blues. The dance floor is packed with young Asian girls shaking it to the beat. Mixed martial-arts fighters spar on the TV above the bar. My focus inevitably returns to the aquarium behind the bar, with eight ordinary goldfish, one sucker fish, and one monster goldfish, rambunctiously badgering its much smaller peers.

After taking the train back downtown, I pass a woman popping a sheet of bubble wrap on one corner. A homeless guy walks with me and asks, "Can I ask you something?"

"What?"

"I'm not going to ask you for no money, like I know a lot of people do down here. Can you buy me a meal?"

I offer him 66¢ instead. "Sorry."

· · · · ·

It's Wednesday morning. A cold front moved in—the locals are freaking out because it's only supposed to hit fifty today.

Over coffee, Wikipedia informs me *Novus ordo seclorum* means "New order for the ages," and *Annuit cœptis* means "God approves our undertakings." The designers of the more famous eagle emblem, William Barton and Charles Thomson, chose the eye-pyramid design as the reverse seal at the request of Congress in 1782. Congress apparently liked the bizarre emblem, which allegedly symbolizes wisdom and a strong national foundation.

Mystery solved. Time to get ready for the day.

I look at myself in the mirror and am not impressed. My T-shirt is too big, I need a belt for my droopy jeans, and my hair is askew. "Come on, dude," I beg. "Pull it together."

I'm a bit lonely, a bit horny, and not feeling too powerful at all. On that note, I head out for the day.

I visit the ArtCar Museum before meeting Dolan Smith, former proprietor-curator of the Museum of the WeirD, at his former house/museum. He had to sell it, he says, because he got married a couple of years ago and moved in with

Cyborg Buck-Bike

his wife, so the city deemed it a commercial property and he can't afford the rigmarole of costs associated with the designation. Now under contract, it's still weird, sure, but now it's an empty house with a Chinese theater in the living room and a sensory deprivation hot tub and the Pet Columbarium in the backyard. The bare walls were once bedecked with all manner of weird artwork, Smith tells me, but most of his paintings have now been moved out or sold off.

Shaking Dolan's hand by his truck, I notice the ladders in the back and ask if he's a contractor. He says he does remodeling jobs around town. "That's how I pay the bills. Nobody wants to buy my art. 'Artists love it'—I tell 'em, 'Then buy it!'"

Next up is the more traditional Menil Collection, showcasing works from the 17,000-piece collection of the late John and Dominique de Menil, a banker and an oil heiress, respectively.

It is truly amazing in its breadth and diversity—ancient relics from the British Isles, Greece, Italy, Africa, and everywhere else, alongside Warhols and Picassos and a wide range of contemporary masterpieces. There is priceless Greek pottery, hyena masks from Mali, a fourteenth-century French virgin and headless child, and an ornately carved Nigerian elephant tusk.

"Be careful, we can't afford to pay for this stuff," warns a woman guiding a group of schoolchildren. Moments later, she leads the group out in a huff. "I'm not going to have something destroyed because you're pushing. We're leaving."

The surrealism room is large and bizarre. There are pieces made from real human skulls from New Guinea. There is a temporary Max Ernst exhibit. A docent tells me his daughter is raising wallabies in Colorado.

All of this stems from Dominique de Menil's inheritance of a fortune generated by Schlumberger, Ltd., which has helped tap the vast oil fields under Texas and beyond. Riches beyond imagination.

Also on the museum's campus—which is free to the public thanks to Dominique de Menil's philanthropic

Jumbo Jack

vision—is the Rothko Chapel. The de Menils commissioned abstract expressionist Mark Rothko to create a sacred place in 1964 and opened it to the public as a place to pray and meditate.

An older African American guy sits behind the front desk.

"How's it going?" I ask him.

"I wish I could tell you," he retorts.

Jumbo Jack

"What?"

"Well, here inside the chapel, it's alright. But out there, where you're coming from, I don't know."

"Houston?" I ask. "The country? The world?"

"All three. I stopped reading the papers. We're fighting over here and we're fighting over there—we can't afford to be fighting at home."

I open the door to the chapel. On the walls hang Rothko's fourteen black and purple paintings. You can't get any more black or purple. I sit on a pillow in the center of the room and meditate on a black canvas.

The floating eye appears in my mind's eye. I dispel it and take a deep breath, but the pyramidal eye reappears time and time again, atop the body of a nude woman, as the Texas Panhandle, a horse's head. Many combine into a spiky 3-D star with a thousand eyes.

I push the eye out of my head and take another deep breath.

Time isn't money. Time is just time.

After a brief stop at the Health Museum, I go back to the hotel. Then I'm off again for another late afternoon walk around downtown Houston, a loop that includes legs in the tunnels below Houston and alongside Buffalo Bayou. The tunnels are busy with people leaving for the day.

Along the bayou I see a homeless man's outdoor bedroom, complete with an office chair.

Back at the hotel bar's free happy hour, I run into the same two Louisiana oil guys and again strike up a conversation. They flew down to Corpus Christi for the day to tour a deepwater oil platform similar to one their company hopes to deploy in the Gulf of Mexico.

Urban bayou

"There's a lot of oil out there, huh?" I ask.

"We hope," says one of them. "Somebody's going to have to put $600 million in up front."

"High risk, high reward," I offer.

"Exactly."

I tell them about Helium-3 and ask about the collapse of oil prices from $150 a barrel to $35 a barrel in late 2008. Another shoe might drop, the second guy warns. The financing "is basically a promise on a promissory note. I don't really understand."

"That's the problem," I retort. "No one person understands the entire big picture."

Stu, the wind-energy guy from Scotland, slides into the bar stool on my left. He tells me that it was basic supply and demand—as demand tanked, the suppliers all played a game of chicken with each other. "Nobody stops pumping, so everybody suffers," he says.

"The US should slap a dollar-a-gallon tax on gas," I say.

Stu concurs. "In Europe, the tax is so high you don't even notice the fluctuations in crude." Again I bring up Helium-3. He dismisses it—the price of oil is too low. There are bigger economic problems than the oil crash, he adds. "The UK doesn't manufacture anything anymore. We're just banking, finance, insurance."

Stu says the world should follow the lead of rural France and Italy. "Money is not that important. Family dinner is hugely important."

We agree that there is a happy medium between socialism and capitalism, that greed-driven corporate fraud has driven the downturn, and that rail projects are worthwhile even if they don't make money. "There's no railway company in history that has ever made money," he says.

Stu says he sees the problems mounting in the United States. "Last night, I saw a woman, well dressed, well put together; she asked me for money. I was spooked. Usually, they're destitute."

We shake hands, he heads for the elevator. I finish my beer and do the same. I change from my jeans and T-shirt into a suit. This is the first time I've put on a suit in several years. I figure I need to project an aura of being rich and powerful. I'm also kind of buzzed from the beer.

But sadly, at the Flying Saucer, I'm as invisible as the night before. I eat dinner and leave. A couple of blocks away, a relatively nicely dressed girl, maybe twenty, runs up to me and asks me for $2 for the train. I turn her down.

Two hours in, I abandon the suit project. Looking back at the panhandler perched awkwardly in the cold, the experiment feels pretty stupid.

I go out for one last beer at Leon's, south of downtown. Ironically, the only people there besides me and the bartender are a guy in a suit and the blond he's romancing.

Okay, so I'm neither rich nor powerful, and I can't even fake it. And I really don't care.

I walk the mile or so back up Main Street, passing a decimated tuxedo rental shop, a desperate horde at the Greyhound station, and a skeletal McDonald's sign, one of several golden arches ravaged by Hurricane Ike I've seen on the trip. A police helicopter flies over the skyline.

If oil truly is our national lifeblood, what happens when the economy has a heart attack?

. . . . .

"Slower Times in the Oil Patch" reads a headline on the front page of the *Houston Chronicle* business section.

I meditate again. My mind is all over the place: work, driving routes, deadlines, women. But at least that fucking eye does not reappear.

After a late checkout, I have lunch at Irma's on the other side of downtown and then drive twenty miles north to the National Museum of Funeral History. En route, a billboard sticks out, Stop Modern Slavery in Houston, with a picture of an enslaved Asian woman.

At the museum, I encounter a novelty coffin artistically impregnated with more than $1,000 worth of bills and coins encapsulated in acrylic for the world to see—at least until the burial.

I fill up my eleven-gallon gas tank, thinking about how that number has changed over the past number of years. When the price of gas topped $4 a gallon, with crude skyrocketing to $150 a barrel, I became obsessed, checking the price multiple times a day online, convinced we were on the verge of peak oil and the catastrophic economic collapse to follow. As the theory goes, once the world's oil production inevitably begins to decline, the market will freak out, sending prices into outer orbit, effectively ending petroleum-based transportation, agriculture, and life as we know it. And then, enter stage left: the cannibal hordes. But it didn't happen, at least not yet.

Taking Patrick's advice, I drive the I-610 loop around the entire city before heading east

The stink of money

to Beaumont, home of the first major oil discovery in Texas, and my final destination on this trip. The loop begins with suburbs that get progressively more posh on the west side of town, culminating in the Galleria, the city's shopping mecca. Then it gets more commercial mixed with pine trees, and I see yet another skeletal, Ike-ravaged golden arches. I get off the loop and head into the heart of Pasadena on Texas Highway 225.

It is truly apocalyptic looking, one petrochemical complex after another as far as the eye can see, topped with belching stacks, plugged into pipelines crisscrossing the bayous, and surrounded by rusted fencing topped with razor wire. The side streets are pitted asphalt, speckled with historical monuments from the Texas Revolution. Gas is 20¢ more than it is in Houston proper, the Food Zone lost all of its letters above the entrance save a lone *o*, and a haggard hooker struts near one complex at 3:41 PM. And Stinkadena indeed: the acrid aroma is so strong I can taste it.

Amidst this galaxy of industry is an island of green, centered on the 567-foot, 70-million-pound icon of Texas independence, the San Jacinto Monument. Erected in 1936 for the centennial celebration of Texas declaring independence from Mexico, the thing is so massive it's very hard to photograph.

Across the road is the *Battleship Texas*, the flagship of the Atlantic fleet in both World War I and II, the first ship to have an aircraft take off from its deck. It was the most powerful boat in the world for several decades, a symbol of the country's military power, now permanently moored here as a museum.

Sometimes, power comes before money, and other times it's money before power. Rarely are they not intertwined.

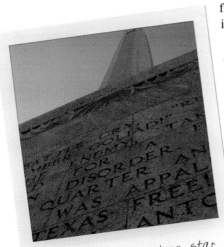

A monument to a lone star

The sunset silhouettes the horror show of a skyline behind me as I drive east toward Beaumont through the swampy, piney exurbs of Houston, under a golden blue sky strung with cottony clouds.

· · · · ·

The next day, I wake up in a hotel room in Beaumont, just west of the Louisiana state line, surrounded by bayous and swampland. It's a crisp, sun-drenched morning.

After starting my final day of the trip with strawberry yogurt and Cheerios, I head downtown.

Beaumont Always Bounces Back! proclaims a billboard, a reference to Ike. There is a detour around roadwork on flood-ravaged streets. The historic center features a nice collection of towers and buildings from the early twentieth century, many of them a reflection of a golden era. It might never be as rosy as it was a century ago, when the first major oil discovery in Texas was going gangbusters here.

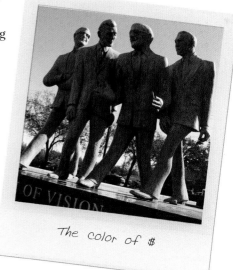

The color of $

Beaumont's population immediately shot up from 9,000 people to 50,000 people after that gusher in 1901. People from all over the country were intrigued by the sheer volume of the black gold underneath the Lone Star State. No one expected it.

In the impressive Texas Energy Museum, the first exhibit begins with a biblical passage, "In the beginning, God created Heaven and the Earth," something the oilmen behind the museum obviously do not believe literally happened in seven days. "Twenty billion years ago," the display continues, "a series of events occurred which gave rise to the universe."

The museum delves deeply into the science of oil and petroleum geology. It all begins with the sun, burning 657 million tons of hydrogen every second, making the *Saturn V* at the Houston Space Center look like a fleeting ember. The sun supported the eons of life on Earth, burying the bottom of ancient seabeds in carbon-rich sediment from all those dead things. Add heat and pressure and plenty of time, and voilà!

To make it simple, after God created heaven and Earth, he created oil.

The museum also explains oil drilling, oil refining, and petrochemical production. A series of plaques look into the history of oil, from its pharmaceutical beginnings in the late 1700s, when whale oil and wood were the country's primary sources of energy, to the coal- and water-powered industrial boom in the subsequent century, to the 1859 discovery of oil in Pennsylvania.

But until the Spindletop find in 1901, there simply wasn't enough oil out there to supply a big market. After Spindletop, there was plenty of it and the market took off, first with Standard Oil dominating, then a whole host of companies emerged, including Beaumont-hatched Gulf and Texaco. Service stations grew like toadstools on the sides of petroleum-based, blacktop roads.

The automobile age began in earnest in the roaring twenties. By 1951, Texas alone produced a billion barrels of oil a year, half of the world's total. However, "Domestic resources did not keep pace with expanding requirements," thus the oil world increasingly turned its attention to the vast seas of oil under the Middle East.

History ends in 1960 on the museum's plaques. Not long after that, the sun began to set on oil production in Texas. The gushers a fading memory, Texas's oil production peaked at 3.5 million barrels a day in the early 1970s. Today it's down about 75 percent from that illustrious high. The decline has been slow and steady, while the world's demand for oil has grown. This particular underground sea of oil is almost dry.

The museum goes on to point out how many consumer products are made with petroleum: a display spotlights

fiber-optic cables, Barbie dolls, golf balls, Juicy Fruit, and plastics of every hue.

In an oil-field diorama upstairs, a mannequin begins talking to me when I press a button, his features emanating from a nearby projector. Introducing himself as Pattillo Higgins, he says that he was sure there was oil under the salt dome known as Spindletop, but nobody would listen. "I told 'em so," he says. "I told 'em so."

His driller, Captain Anthony Lucas, is represented by the next dummy. "This great well gushed 100,000 barrels a day in a great black stream, 200 feet high," he says. Once they figured out how to cap the thing ten days later, the rig was surrounded by "a lake of a million barrels of oil."

On my way out, the elderly volunteer woman at the front desk warns me to be careful driving. "There's a lot of nuts out there."

My final stop may as well have been the moon in 1899, when oil was pretty much the day's Helium-3. Nobody quite knew what to do with it, mostly because they never had much of it.

I'm greeted by Myrtle in the Spindletop gift shop. "This is where the oil industry was born," she says. "They called it Swindletop for a while. When there's money to be made, you're going to get all kinds coming in."

She tells me that the field produced for ten years, then it was dry. Spindletop became a ghost town. "Back when the gusher went off, oil was 3¢ a barrel," she adds. "Water was $6 a barrel because everybody needed water."

Myrtle also tells me more about Pattillo, how people called him the fool and the millionaire,

Bits of the past

how he was a reformed, one-armed, hell-raiser who taught Sunday school classes. He was right about the oil, of course, but he was also cut out of the fattest deal by his business partner, Lucas.

"Look at World War II—we wouldn't have won it without all of this oil," she adds. I'm just glad Hitler wasn't from Texas.

Outside, a weathered boomtown of storefronts presents life at Spindletop a century before. There's a saloon, a stable, an undertaker, a printing shop, a mercantile, a board of trade to handle all of the wheeling and dealing, and a pair of requisite drilling towers. But the place is empty, except for me and a couple of tourists. All of the other people are cruising by at sixty miles an hour on the highway a hundred yards away. I was just on it a few minutes ago and will be back on it a few minutes ahead. Personally, I'd be pretty much useless without unleaded gasoline.

Spindletop may be no more, but the oil age continues to roll—and all that comes with it, bad and good no end in sight.

Where to go...

La Torretta Del Lago Resort & Spa
600 La Torretta Blvd., Montgomery
936-448-4400
www.latorrettadellago
resortandspa.com

Houston Space Center
1601 NASA Pkwy., Houston
281-244-2100
www.spacecenter.org

The Magnolia Hotel
1100 Texas Ave., Houston
888-915-1110
www.magnoliahotelhouston.com

Reef
2600 Travis St., Houston
713-526-8282
www.reefhouston.com

La Carafe
813 Congress St., Houston
713-229-9399

Orange Show Center for Visionary Art
2402 Munger St., Houston
713-926-6368
www.orangeshow.org

Beer Can House
222 Malone St., Houston
www.beercanhouse.org

Wabash Feed Antiques and Feed
5701 Washington Ave., Houston
713-863-8322
www.wabashfeed.com

Howard Hughes Gravesite
Glenwood Cemetery
2525 Washington Ave., Houston
713-864-7886
www.glenwoodcemetery.org

SculpturWorx
(Home of the big presidential heads)
2500 Summer St., Houston

Lankford Grocery & Market
88 Dennis St., Houston
713-522-9555

The Flower Man
2305 Francis St., Houston

Blaffer Gallery
On the campus of the University of Houston
120 Fine Arts Bldg., Houston
713-743-9521
www.class.uh.edu/blaffer

Enron Building
1400 Smith St., Houston

**Flying Saucer Draught
Emporium**
705 Main St., Houston
713-228-7468
www.beerknurd.com

Continental Club
3700 Main St., Houston
713-529-9899
www.continentalclub.com

ArtCar Museum
140 Heights Blvd., Houston
713-861-5526
www.artcarmuseum.com

**Menil Collection/
Rothko Chapel**
1515 Sul Ross St., Houston
713-525-9400
www.menil.org

**The Health Museum's
Amazing Body Pavilion**
1515 Hermann Dr., Houston
713-521-1515
www.thehealthmuseum.org

Leon's Lounge
1006 Mcgowen St., Houston
713-659-3052

Irma's
22 N. Chenevert St., Houston
713-222-0767

**National Museum of
Funeral History**
415 Barren Springs Dr., Houston
281-876-3063
www.nmfh.org

Pasadena
Just east of Houston
www.ci.pasadena.tx.us

San Jacinto Monument
1 Monument Cir., La Porte
281-479-2421
www.sanjacinto-museum.org

Texas Energy Museum
600 Main St., Beaumont
409-833-5100
www.texasenergymuseum.org

**Spindletop-Gladys City
Boomtown Museum**
US 69 at University Dr.,
Beaumont
409-835-0823
www.spindletop.org

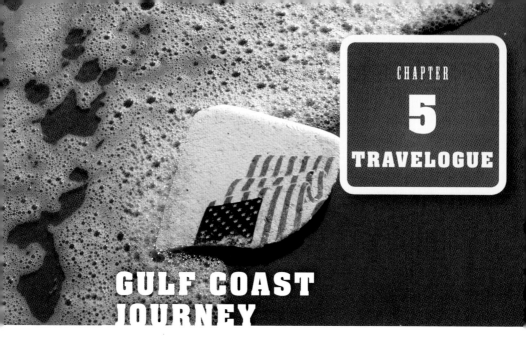

GULF COAST JOURNEY

FIVE DAYS, 500 MILES

"Having trouble with hurricane insurance claims?" blares a radio ad. "Call 1-800-TX-LAWYER now!"

I'm driving through a nondescript neighborhood in Port Arthur, the easternmost city on the Texas Gulf Coast. Well, it would be nondescript except for the fact that I see houses with blue tarps covering all or part of their roofs. Hurricane Ike swept through like a buzz saw, leaving a swath of destruction—and little else—in its wake. That swath is still apparent today. The next ad on the radio pitches new roofs. A Progressive Insurance Jeep turns the corner in front of me.

I drive down to the waterfront, in this case the Sabine-Neches Ship Channel between Texas and Louisiana, and get out of the car. The cool coastal breeze hits me like a gaseous quaalude. It feels really good just to take a deep breath. But it's already the afternoon and I've got a busy agenda. No time to gawk at the boats.

The water parallels my drive west to downtown Port Arthur and the Museum of the Gulf Coast, which focuses on the oil industry and the Gulf's ecosystem. The state's record flounder, thirteen pounds and with one eye bizarrely migrated to the top of its head (standard for flounder), is behind Plexiglas. Other displays cover the brackish estuaries, the slow-moving bayous, the moon-driven tides, the sometimes-oppressive humidity, and the Gulf Coast's diverse wildlife habitats, populated by shrimp and gators and birds and frogs.

The cultural-history exhibits begin with explorer Álvarez de Pineda mapping the Gulf Coast in 1519 and reporting giants and dwarves on the mainland as he claimed it for the Spanish crown.

The following century, the Spanish established missions along the coast, complete with soldiers to enforce the holy men's preachings and fight off the British and the French. Then you have Mexican independence in 1820, Texan independence in 1836, followed by statehood and the Civil War.

A wall is dedicated to the third coast's indigenous people, emphasizing the Atakapa tribe. Choctaw for "man eaters," the Atakapa lived in the area until a few hundred years ago, harvesting shellfish, bird eggs, wild potatoes, and gators—which they hunted for their meat, skin, and oil.

"The rancid smell from the oil helped repulse outsiders," the exhibit informs.

Next is the Atakapa legend of Kisselpoo, a princess born under a full moon and thusly protected by the Moon Goddess. Her family wanted her to marry an aging chieftain, but she fell in love with an unacceptable stranger. On the night of a full moon when her arranged marriage was set to take place, she fled with the stranger on a canoe. The chief's medicine man invoked the wrath of the gods, a storm overturned the canoe, and Kisselpoo and the stranger disappeared into the moonlit water forever.

Torn appart

This of course did not sit too well with the Moon Goddess, who asked her brother, the Storm God, to whip up a devastating hurricane—which he did, wiping away every trace of the village. The moral: don't piss off the Moon Goddess.

Another display informs me that the Atakapa had the nasty habit of eating one of their own after an unsuccessful hunt. A Frenchman in the 1700s reported seeing some miffed hunters decapitating one among them and cannibalizing him on the spot. Don't ask me how they selected the eatee.

On my way out—after visiting the Janis Joplin shrine and Robert Rauschenberg gallery upstairs—I notice some interpretive displays on hurricanes I missed the first time around. "Hurricanes are great circular counterclockwise motions of air that derive their energy from air rising off warm ocean waters," reads one of them.

A Bible found in receding floodwaters is mounted aside photos of the 1915 hurricane that devastated Port Arthur. It was said to be even more ferocious than the 1900 storm that decimated Galveston, killing 6,000 people, still the most deadly natural disaster in US history.

From the museum, I make an inland beeline west to the little town of Winnie and drop back to the waterfront on the Bolivar Peninsula. This area took the brunt of Ike. It looks like it could have happened last week. Few houses remain, only foundations and pilings and stilts, the occasional bent gate. Piles of wreckage are everywhere—furniture, appliances, toys, clothing, even cars.

There is a neighborhood with one lone last house standing, surrounded by the remnants of dozens of structures that weren't so lucky. A billboard by the side of the road dubs it The Survivor. Another old house was torn from its foundation and ended up on the side of the road. Most stores were reduced to rubble.

It's like somebody took a quaint coastal town and shook it up in a snow globe. Once the water quieted down, everything settled in a different place. But instead of fake plastic snowflakes, they're little tiny pieces of people's lives.

My timing is perfect to catch the free ferry across to Galveston Island.

Across from the beach at a bar called the Poop Deck, Texas drawlers comment on the surfers riding the waves across the street.

I ask the bartender about the storm. She says the bar stayed open. "We don't evacuate—we intoxicate!" she proudly explains. "If you don't like the weather, stick around—it's gonna change."

She gives me directions to the memorial to the victims of the 1900 hurricane, one of few waterfront statues that

Totally destroyed

survived Ike, and asks me what inspires me to write. After my glib response, she tells me she started to write poetry while serving three years in prison. "I can only write when there is nothing occupying my mind and I am sitting perfectly still," she says. I tell her I'm pretty much the opposite.

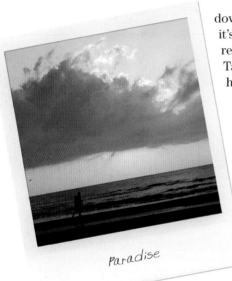

Paradise

After a quick driving tour of downtown and a walk on the beach, it's time for me to move. I've got a reservation for a room at the historic Tarpon Inn in Port Aransas, three hours or so south, and it's nearly 5 PM.

I make my way out of the city and drive south, mildly surprised at how good of shape the buildings are in, considering the relative condition of those on the Bolivar Peninsula.

But my southward momentum comes to an abrupt stop a half hour south of town when I encounter a Road Closed sign in the middle of my lane. It seems the road was reclaimed by the sea. Backtracking to Galveston, I notice much more damage than I did on my first pass. Massive flocks of birds are out in search of dinner. A house is missing a wall, but a bed and chairs are still in place.

The sun is setting by the time I get back to town. I should have stayed here. What was I thinking? It's too late to cancel the reservation. I drive into the inky night, below the Cheshire grin of the moon and past dazzlingly lit petrochemical palaces.

But the route I pick turns out to be remarkably slow. Every stoplight seems to turn red on my approach. I take a wrong turn in Aransas Pass. Cranky, tired, and disheveled, I finally get to the Tarpon Inn around 11 PM. No one is there. I call the posted number. No answer. I leave a message.

Purgatory

What am I doing? Why did I not stay in Galveston? I'm supposed to be a travel writer delivering sage advice and telling an intriguing story. Who in their right mind would take this kind of a trip?

A few minutes pass and the innkeeper calls me back. "I was in the tub," she apologizes, and tells me my key is in the door. It's a positive step, but I'm still frazzled. I decide to go out for a beer, and a sports car makes like it's going to run me over in the first crosswalk. After dodging safely to the other side, I'm too dejected to even drink. I go back to the hotel, feeling sorry for myself, cursing.

That's when I read the historic marker out front, about how a hurricane destroyed the place and it was rebuilt, and how another hurricane meant it was only accessible by boat for a spell.

Despite my mistakes and lack of planning, it was a pretty good day. There was no hurricane, nor am I the unlucky Atakapa hunter being ripped asunder by my pals and eaten raw. It's not even hurricane season—and cannibalism is out of vogue—but let's keep things in perspective. It was a good day.

· · · · ·

A late start is first on the agenda the next morning. Coffee is in the lobby, now unlocked. The wall behind the coffeepot is plastered with what at first appear to be leaves, each of them bearing a signature and a date. Then I recall the mention of tarpon scales on the historical marker: Port

Aransas was the Tarpon Fishing Capital of the World and the Tarpon Inn was its flagship hotel. FDR fished here, as did many other notables. The tradition emerged at the inn for successful anglers to nail on the wall a signed scale from their catch. Thousands of tarpon scales now cover it from floor to ceiling. FDR's and other celebrity scales are kept in their own glass cases.

Once fully caffeinated, I decide to walk down to the beach before my scheduled dolphin-watching excursion with Deep Sea Adventures at 1:30 PM. The sun is a shining button in the clear blue sky. The paved road winds through grassy dunes and ends on a bustling beach. The lack of pavement doesn't stop the cars from arriving in droves, parking, and relieving themselves of families, retired couples, and fishing buddies by the dozen.

I take off my flip-flops and step into the first tide my bare feet have touched in eight months. The cool water immediately tranquilizes me, beating its steady rhythm of tides, thanks to Kisselpoo's Moon Goddess. There's nothing like the ocean, its blue tentacles cradling the entire planet. That's why the hurricanes don't really matter. Some people just need the sea.

My camera battery runs out of juice, so I head back to the Tarpon Inn to charge it for a few minutes before dolphin watching. I turn my cell phone off and put on my tennis shoes before heading out the door a half hour later.

Gary at Deep Sea Adventures says he tried to call me about how his tour was merged with another group from another company

Seahorses of different Colors

that went out a half hour earlier. In other words, I missed the boat.

"How hard is it to catch a tarpon?" I ask, setting my sights on perhaps adding a scale to the wall at the inn.

But Gary dashes my dreams. "Really hard," he says. "They're mostly in Florida. This used to be the Tarpon Capital of the World in the 1930s."

"What happened? Did they get overfished?"

"No, they actually go to spawn in Mexico and they would throw out nets across the rivers and catch thousands of them. They would fill up dump trucks and use them as fertilizer."

Regardless, my timing is off for the dolphin trip, and a deep-sea fishing trip is out of my budget. This is beginning to feel like the world's most poorly executed road trip. Again a bit despondent, I dash across the street to the visitor center and ask the girl there for advice.

After a couple of false starts, she finds me the perfect afternoon activity in my budget. "There's a ferry you can take to this uninhabited island, St. Jo," she says. "People go over to fish and find shells and beachcomb. All kinds of stuff wash up on the beach."

She hands me an enticing pirate-themed brochure with the jetty boat schedule. Apparently, Jean Lafitte, the nineteenth-century French pirate who earned the nickname The Terror of the Gulf of Mexico, buried a diamond-encrusted dagger someplace on the island. And it could be cursed.

Next boat leaves at 2:00—in twenty minutes. I go back to my room, hit the convenience store next door for some Flamin' Hot Fritos and a twenty-four-ounce tall boy of Lone Star. I make it to the ferry with five minutes to spare. It's a ten-minute ride to the creaky dock at St. Jo Island.

Disembarking, most everyone has a fishing pole and heads straight up the jetty. I break from the herd, taking a left and walking north up the beach.

I walk through a jumble of plastic bottles, gallon jugs, and buckets onto the beach proper. There are boats moored a mile off the shore, entering and exiting the ship channel to the harbor. There are gulls, but not a human in sight.

It is shocking just how much stuff is here. The plastic containers are just the beginning. There are half-buried juice bottles and foil pouches of food powder, both undergoing natural processes nature never intended.

Time-out at St. Jo

There is something jutting from the surf up ahead—an ancient metal wheel covered in barnacles and algae. Farther up, a wooden patio chair, its legs and seat sunk under the sand.

Next is a patio table, previously rigged flat with an upside-down trash can, and two upside-down buckets for chairs. One of them has four empty tall boys next to it. Nice. I take a seat and crack my own tall boy. A crusty starfish is on the table. I see a barbecue brush over there, a boot, some driftwood.

But it's still a beach on a sunny day. The sound of the tides still soothes, the ocean air is still exhilarating to breathe, and I still like to walk in the surf barefoot.

Up ahead, I see a barrier extending into the sea—a barbwire fence. A man is on the other side, working his way up the dunes that front the beach. He disappears from view, then reappears amidst the dunes on my side of the fence.

We talk. He's George, a retiree who spends the cold Colorado winter down here with his wife, Janice, who's just behind. He tells me that last year he saw a chunk of a helicopter just up ahead and points to some lawn chairs on the horizon. "This goes on for twenty-five or thirty miles," he adds, noting that it's cattle ranchland owned by famed Fort Worth tycoons the Bass brothers.

I squiggle under a smooth segment of the fence and make my way toward the chairs, saying hello to Janice en route.

There's a plastic Halloween pumpkin and a hard hat covered in oil-rig safety stickers.

The white plastic chairs are perfect to kick back and finish my beer, complete with a flipped over milk crate to set my drink on.

It's 3:15. I'm at a crossroads. I need to turn around if I want to catch the 4:10 ferry back to town. Or I can continue up the beach and catch the last ferry of the day at 6:10. Storm clouds are threatening. I decide to press on. Maybe I'll find Lafitte's cursed diamond dagger.

Come here often?

I start to pick up shells and sand dollars, keeping my eye out for anything else of value. I also play the alphabet game, looking on the beach for objects beginning with letters A through Z.

Aerosol can, Battery, Chair, Deodorant, Egg carton, Flipper, Garbage bags, Hard hat, Ice chest (Styrofoam), Junk of all kinds, Ketchup bottle, Lighthouse (miniature, decorative, wood), Margarine tub, Nails (rusty, jutting from plank)...

I take a piss and climb up a dune. The interior is a wild and rugged grassland, a different world. Where was I? Oh, yeah, O.

Oil can, Propane tank, Q—I'll come back to that one, Refrigerator door, Sand (lots), Television set (three, in fact), Unopened five-gallon jug of water (seal intact), Vinyl scraps, Whiskey bottle, X—pass, Yellow nylon rope, Z—another pass.

Q, X, and Z? All I need is a quill, and an X-ray machine, and a zebra-print anything, and I'm golden. And it wouldn't shock me.

It starts to intermittently drizzle. There is an ancient hulking, rusting boiler, perhaps a half ton, stuck in the mud.

There's that helicopter wreckage, out twenty feet in the surf. An old hot-water heater. And a pleasure boat, long since ransacked and full of beer cans. As much as there is on the sand, I bet what's under it is even more amazing.

I turn around at 4:30 and make it back to the dock with time to spare. The raindrops stop, dolphins rise for air, birds dive for fish, and big boats chug out to sea. My booty: five shells, two sand dollars, and that sticker-clad hard hat I saw next to the plastic jack-o'-lantern. Sure, no diamond-encrusted dagger, but easily worth my $12 ticket.

It's just me and four teenagers—three in T-shirts with fishing poles, one in a wet suit, spear gun in hand—on the last boat back to Port Aransas, the sun setting over St. Jo's lonely seashore of the damned.

· · · · ·

The long walk on the beach makes for a good and long night's rest.

Before I check out, I ask about the tarpon scales in the lobby. The last one went up four years ago, the clerk tells me. Most of them are from the 1930s.

Dos patos

I head to a birding spot on the fringes of town, the Leona Belle Turnbull Birding Center, the consummate wetlands environment centered on a shallow pond full of ducks and turtles. A chubby rodent known as a nutria sleeps in the sun on the edge of the marsh, its whiskers stirring. A flock of pinkish birds, roseate spoonbills, rest a short distance away. Signs warn of alligators, but none make their presence known on this sunny morning. Apparently, an eleven-footer calls the place home.

The idyllic scene is a marked contrast to the chaos of St. Jo Island.

Likewise, it's almost too nice at Padre Island National Seashore, a half-hour drive south of Port Aransas. This is the longest undeveloped stretch of barrier island in the world: fifty miles of sand and dunes and no condos.

I talk to Chelsea, the ranger working the visitor center, and ask her what to do at the seashore if you have no fishing pole or four-wheel drive vehicle. She suggests walking on the beach and tells me I might see some interesting stuff that's washed ashore. I tell her about St. Jo Island and ask her why all the TVs and buckets and whatnot end up in this area.

She pulls out a map of the Gulf. "There's just one inlet and one little outlet, and all of the currents go here," she explains. Indeed, arrows from Cuba, Mexico, Florida, and elsewhere point straight at the central Texas coast. "After Ike, people's homes were washing up here." Volunteer crews regularly clean up the man-made junk that ends up at the national seashore.

Out on the beach, I walk a few miles south. The crowd is sparse, the sun is shining, and the water beckons. When nobody is looking, I strip naked and submerge myself in the shallow surf. It feels incredible. I let a wave or two pass over me. The water is cool, catalytic. Baptized by the Gulf, I run back to my stuff, hastily pull my shorts back on, and sit on the shore, hypnotized by wave after wave after wave crashing into froth.

Are the patterns of water chaos? Or are they destiny?

It couldn't be nicer. All I can see is sand and sea and sun and sky. It's that simple.

The Gulf

Back at the visitor center, Chelsea is gone, but a different ranger tells me about sea-turtle recovery on the island. In the late 1970s, Kemp's ridley sea turtles—animals that once arrived en masse to lay eggs on Padre Island—were verging on extinction. Mexico and the United States teamed up on a recovery program, gathering eggs from nests on the island to incubate in Galveston. It's working: officials released 800 hatchlings in 1998 and more than 11,000 in 2008.

After stopping at Snoopy's Pier under the JFK Causeway for a shrimp sandwich and a side of hush puppies, I cruise into downtown Corpus Christi, nearly as sedate as Padre Island this Super Bowl Sunday. I watch most of the game in my room at the Omni Bayfront, dashing up to the rooftop bar for the final few minutes.

· · · · ·

The next morning I visit the Texas State Aquarium at Corpus Christi Beach, a touristy area complete with motels, T-shirt shops, and seafood restaurants, all with at least a hint of nautical kitsch.

The sea horses entrance me. Three species live in the Gulf of Mexico but they are very rare. It seems the souvenir industry has all but wiped them out. "During pregnancy, the female sea horse places her eggs in his pouch where they are fertilized by his sperm," an exhibit informs. I watch one eating, hanging onto a reed with its prehensile tail. Amazing. The sea turtles and jellyfish also captivate my brain.

I watch the dolphin show and learn that they like Jell-O and also learn of a Greek myth: a dolphin convinced the sea nymph Amphitrite to marry the sea god Poseidon and was thus granted a dolphin-shaped constellation. It's kind of like Kisselpoo, without the handsome stranger and the wrath of the gods.

There is also a wall-mounted discussion of dolphins for thousands of years coming to the rescue of humans in trouble at sea. "Do these traditions mean that dolphins have extraordinary intelligence? Do we yearn for their ability to live in an environment that seems mysterious and inhospitable to humans?"

Do they feel the same way about us?

Next door to the aquarium is the hulking USS *Lexington,* an aircraft carrier that sunk a million tons of enemy ships during World War II, now moored permanently at Corpus Christi Beach as a museum. It was the first foreign boat to enter Tokyo Harbor at the end of World War II and served as a training vessel in the Gulf during the 1970s and 1980s before the Navy took it out of service in 1991.

In a World War II history gallery, I learn the term *kamikaze* originates from a Japanese wind god who took out a Mongol horde with a typhoon. After checking out the flight deck and the bridge, I rush through the bowels—home to the crew's bunks, the barber shop, the engine room, the dentist's office, and the mess hall—and off the ship to have lunch at Pier 99 with Patti of the local tourism bureau.

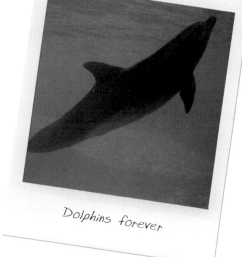

Dolphins forever

A lifelong Corpus Christi–area resident, Patti tells me her memories of Hurricane Celia making landfall near the city in 1970. "Back then we didn't evacuate," she says. "I saw fear in my father's face for the first time, and that scared me." But after it was over, there was a sense of community, she adds. Everyone shared food, water, kitchens, and whatever still worked. "For a ten-year-old girl, it was a lot of fun. We really got to know our neighbors."

After the fried oyster platter, I head back downtown and walk a long loop. A bay-front historic marker informs me that a 1554 hurricane shipwrecked a trio of Spanish treasure galleons on Padre Island, earning it the nickname The Graveyard of Ships. At the Port of Corpus Christi (the fifth largest in the country), a security guard chastises me for taking photos. Doesn't she think a terrorist would use a hidden camera? Cursing, I head south, turning around to take a picture in spite, ending up at the Texas Surf Museum in the back of Surf Club Records.

The temporary exhibit covers the state's surfing women—dubbed "Fallopian Tubes"—and a permanently installed re-creation of a 1970s teenage surfer's bedroom, featuring a shag comforter, Pong game, and poster of Corpus Christi native daughter Farrah Fawcett.

I learn that Texas surfers love the big waves that accompany hurricanes. "People don't surf the storm, they surf the edges of the storm," the guy behind the cash register tells me. "Even in California, the big waves are coming from a storm someplace."

The pictures of surfing girls and the endless blue remind me: I need to get back to the beach one more time. Tomorrow is my last day on the Gulf Coast.

But once again my plans are lacking. I have none.

I go out for beers and dinner at the Executive Surf Club. It's a fun joint. A huge deep-sea lure replica hangs above the bar. There's a good crowd for a Monday.

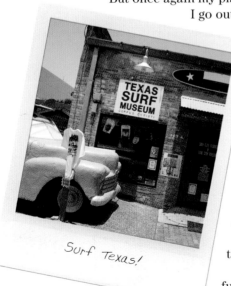

Surf Texas!

"Tomorrow, I don't know—I could drive down to South Padre," I wonder aloud after a shrimp wrap and two and a half Shiner Bock drafts. "Or I could just hang out around here, go to the beach, and go to Austin tomorrow night."

"I would do that," says a teenaged busboy out of nowhere.

Who the hell are you, kid? I'm a fucking travel writer—don't you think I know what I'm doing? Wait. I don't.

The kid is right. Beach in the morning; Austin by nightfall. Home in forty-eight hours.

I only have one day. Might as well spend as much of it on the beach as possible.

· · · · ·

It's nicer than perfect the next day at the national seashore. The crowd is even sparser than it was two days earlier. A half mile from the parking lot is pure solitude.

I strip down and again submerge myself below the tide. I may not be back to any beach for the better part of a year. Damn.

Then I cross my legs on a beach towel and decide to meditate. Lingering regrets about not planning the trip well fracture my concentration.

"Come on," I say aloud. "There are some things you can't control. You're on the beach. It's a beautiful day. Relax."

I close my eyes. A deep breath. Lukewarm water rushes past my ankles and into my lap.

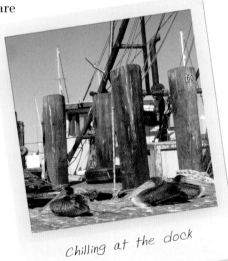

Shit! The tide! My camera! My notepad! My jacket! Moron!

The world's most poorly executed road trip continues.

Alas, my things get wet, but nothing is lost. My camera hiccups but still functions.

Yes, there are some things you can't control. And when you fuck up, if at all possible, go to the beach.

Chilling at the dock

Where to go...

Museum of the Gulf Coast
700 Procter St., Port Arthur
409-982-7000
www.museumofthegulfcoast.org

Poop Deck
2928 Seawall Blvd., Galveston
409-763-9151

1900 Hurricane Memorial
48th St. and
Seawall Blvd., Galveston

Tarpon Inn
200 E. Cotter Ave.,
Port Aransas
361-749-5555
www.thetarponinn.com

Jetty Boat to St. Jo
San Jose Island
Fisherman's Wharf
361-749-5448
www.jettyboat.net

Leona Belle Turnbull
Birding Center
South end of Ross Ave.,
Port Aransas

Padre Island
National Seashore
Southeast of Corpus Christi
361-949-8068
www.nps.gov/pais

Snoopy's Pier
Under the JFK Causeway
at 13313 S. Padre Island Dr.,
Corpus Christi
361-949-8815

Texas State Aquarium
2710 N. Shoreline Blvd.,
Corpus Christi
800-477-4853
www.texasstateaquarium.org

USS *Lexington*
2914 N. Shoreline Blvd.,
Corpus Christi
800-523-9539
www.usslexington.com

Pier 99
2822 N. Shoreline Blvd.
361-887-0764

Texas Surf Museum
309 N. Water St., next to
Exec Surf Club,
Corpus Christi
361-888-7873
www.texassurfmuseum.com

Executive Surf Club
309 N. Water St.,
Corpus Christi
361-884-7873
www.executivesurfclub.com

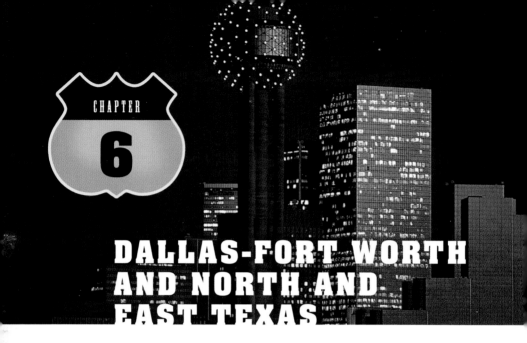

DALLAS-FORT WORTH AND NORTH AND EAST TEXAS

INTRODUCTION

Surrounded by plains and swamps and woodlands, and separated from Oklahoma by the serpentine Red River, this chunk of Texas is perfectly centered on the mega metroplex of Dallas-Fort Worth.

The ninth largest city in the country, Dallas is a sprawling, sturdy, and ruthlessly efficient metropolis, with historic neighborhoods encircling a redeveloped core of shining corporate castles in the full spectrum of shapes and metallic hue. It is one of the few cities that has no good reason for its location—no confluence of rivers or cradling valley. The Trinity River is there, sure, but Dallas-Fort Worth is the largest metro area in the country without a navigable link to the sea. It's pretty much where it's at because the city fathers said the spot was as good as any.

Some people have said Dallas isn't sure if it wants to be Paris or New York City, but it's actually more like Amsterdam in reverse, clean and orderly and well behaved. Others say it's a bit too clean and organized, antiseptic even, but those folks clearly are in need of a weekend-long bender in funky old Deep Ellum.

On the extreme western end of this sprawling Tex-urban spectrum, Fort Worth is an old-fashioned cow town cross-bred with a modern American city that all but encourages misbehavior. Booze, and I believe swearing and spitting, are allowed in the streets at the Stockyards National Historic District, formerly a thriving stockyard district but now frequented by more tourists and drunks than cows. Bars dot the slickly preserved historic downtown, and there's a certain devilishness in the air all over the city. Or maybe that's just the cattle.

Rural East Texas is perhaps a little weird, and it gets weirder yet the closer you get to the Louisiana state line.

STATS & FACTS

- **Dallas has more shopping centers per capita than any other American city.**

- **Dallas/Fort Worth International Airport is larger than Manhattan.**

- **The largest oil field in the United States, the East Texas Oil Field, has produced more than 5 billion barrels of oil since its discovery in 1930.**

- **In 1971, Dallas restaurateur Mariano Martinez invented the frozen margarita machine, modifying a soft-serve ice cream machine. It is now part of the Smithsonian's collection.**

- **The Fort Worth Herd goes on the world's only daily cattle drive at 11:30 am and 4 pm through the streets of the stockyards.**

Moss-draped Caddo Lake is a remote and eerie place that's allegedly the home of Texas's Bigfoot, and a town called Uncertain is its main port. Names aside, I'm certain that this is one of the state's oddest crannies.

BIG THINGS AND OTHER ROAD ART

World's Largest Armadillo
Fall Creek Farms, 6920 Fall Creek Hwy., near Acton
817-910-9232
www.upicktx.com

After getting his start at Six Flags Over Texas in Arlington, the Killer has retired to a more pastoral lifestyle at Fall Creek Farms. Welder extraordinaire Marc Rankin has created a number of sculptures on outdoor display across Texas, but his rendition of the state mammal is certainly among his most superlative: this 48-foot long, 9,000-pound 'dillo is in fact certified by the *Guinness Book* people as the largest in the world. While you're here, you can not only gawk at Killer, but you can also pick yourself some peaches, strawberries, and organic veggies.

Eiffel Tower in a Cowboy Hat
At the Love Civic Center,
Jefferson Rd. and Collegiate Dr., Paris

This sixty-five-foot replica of the Eiffel Tower resides in the lesser-known city of Paris—Texas, that is. Nobody seems to know who named the city or why they named it, but the prevailing theory is that Paris, Texas, is named for Paris, France. Originally built in 1993 by the local chapter of a boilermakers' union, this Eiffel Tower is no threat to the 1,063-foot original—but does size really matter when it comes to American copies

Read:

- *The Last Picture Show* by Larry McMurtry
- *Libra* by Don DeLillo
- *Baja Oklahoma* by Dan Jenkins

Listen:

- Anything by Deep Ellum blues legends Blind Lemon Jefferson and Blind Willie Johnson
- *Cowboys from Hell* by Pantera
- Keep in mind that Vanilla Ice, Jessica and Ashlee Simpson, and Meat Loaf all hail from Dallas

Watch:

- JFK
- Bonnie and Clyde
- Walker, Texas Ranger

To-Do Checklist:

- Come up with a novel conspiracy theory
- Bleed silver and blue
- Go all Wild West in Fort Worth

of European landmarks? In 1998, local leaders topped the tower in the second-largest Paris in the world with an oversized cowboy hat—presumably in response to rumors that the Paris across the pond was going to top the real thing with a humongous beret.

Very Tall Giraffe
At the Dallas Zoo, 650 S.R.L. Thornton Fwy.
214-670-5656
www.dallaszoo.com

A tribute to the zoo's snaky-necked ungulates, the sixty-seven-and-a-half-foot giraffe in front of the Dallas Zoo is the tallest statue in Texas—by a tongue. The 1997 work of Bob Cassilly extends its prehensile tongue skyward past the peak elevation of Sam Houston's head in Huntsville, beating the Texan hero by a mere six inches. Rumor has it that the tongue isn't the Houston-beater, but a wispy blade of grass that's perched atop it.

R.I.P.

Tom Landry, 1924–2000
Sparkman Hillcrest Memorial Park
7405 W. Northwest Hwy., Dallas

The living embodiment of Texas football, Tom Landry transcended the game. His iconic fedora hat, two Super Bowl coaching wins, and streak of twenty winning seasons are all legendary. But many forget his true coaching genius was innovating the game: he invented the four-three defense and the middle linebacker position, and he brought back the shotgun and man-in-motion, both discarded in earlier decades. If you aren't a football fan, your eyes are probably glazed over now. Thank you for your patience.

Billy the Kid, 1859–1881 (Or Was It 1950?)

Billy the Kid Museum
114 N. Pecan St., Hico
254-796-2523
www.billythekidmuseum.com

Local legend has it that Henry McCarty (a.k.a. William H. Bonney, a.k.a. Henry Antrim, a.k.a. infamous western gunfighter Billy the Kid) wasn't shot dead by Pat Garrett in New Mexico in 1881, but escaped to live a full life in Hico, Texas, dropping dead on the sidewalk in this quaint town in 1950 at the ripe old age of ninety-one. As the story goes, a fellow named Brushy Bill Roberts fessed up that he was really Billy the Kid, and Garrett had just killed a guy who looked like him. In his last years, Roberts claimed the governor of New Mexico had reneged on a promise to pardon

him in 1878, so he went on the run after his widely reported demise, assuming a new identity. But when old Brushy Bill died of a heart attack on his way to the post office in Hico in 1950, the controversy began, local leaders grabbed onto it, and the tale is now covered in a museum in downtown Hico and on markers posted around town.

Stevie Ray Vaughan, 1954–1990

Laurel Land Memorial Park
6000 S.R.L. Thornton Fwy., Dallas

Born in Dallas but raised all over Texas, Stevie Ray Vaughan started playing a three-string plastic toy guitar when he was nine years old. He spent hours listening to and re-creating the

blues in his room and was playing in rock bands by the age of twelve. When he was seventeen, he dropped out of high school in Dallas and moved to Austin, where he played clubs until closing time and slept on a barroom pool table afterward. He finally hit the big time in the early 1980s, lived a decadent rock-and-roll lifestyle until kicking coke and booze in 1986, and then wrote hits about his rough road to sobriety, including "Tightrope" and "Crossfire." The latter was his only mainstream hit, topping the charts in 1989, a year before the helicopter crash that claimed his life. Two decades later, Vaughan remains one of the icons of Texas blues guitar, riffs from his fiery Stratocaster still echoing through the sound of more artists than you can count.

Bonnie Parker, 1910–1934, and Clyde Barrow, 1909–1934

Bonnie, Crown Hill Memorial Park
9700 Webb Chapel Rd., Dallas

Clyde, Western Heights Cemetery
1617 Fort Worth Ave., Dallas

It's the familiar old story: boy meets girl, they fall in love and go on a murderous crime spree before a posse of cops take them out in a hail of bullets. Short (four-foot-eleven), strong-willed Bonnie Parker met petty criminal Clyde Barrow in 1930, and they immediately fell in love. Their robbery exploits include gas stations and convenience stores, but also a number of banks from 1932 to 1934. The gang killed nine police officers and deservedly earned the enmity of the Texas Rangers, who ambushed them and filled them with lead on May 23, 1934, just east of the Louisiana state line. Interestingly, Bonnie never fired a shot during the spree and Clyde was after vengeance, not fortune: the gang's run was an act of revenge against the Texas prison system that initially locked him up in 1926 for turning in a rental car too late. That's one argument for lenience.

Old Rip, 1890s–1933
Eastland County Courthouse
100 W. Main St., Eastland

Enthusiastic but cruel, the founders of Eastland, Texas, entombed a horned toad in the cornerstone of the Eastland County Courthouse when construction began in 1897. A new courthouse replaced it in 1928, and the cornerstone was cracked open in the process of demolition. To everybody's surprise, Old Rip (as in Van Winkle) was alive—or that's the story that became legend, to be later adapted into cartoons and tall tales and publicity stunts. Of course, the lizard died less than a year later. In 1997, Governor Dubya said Old Rip had "true Texas grit" on the 100th anniversary of his entombment. Old Rip's nicely preserved body is on display in a miniature coffin in the front window of the courthouse and is commemorated by a city park bearing an oversized sculpture of the rugged Lazarus of a reptile.

VICE

Fort Worth Nightlife

Everything, of course, is bigger in Texas, and honky-tonks don't get any bigger than Billy Bob's Texas (2520 Rodeo Plz. in the Historic Stockyards, www.billybobstexas.com).

Housed in a former cattle barn, the 127,000-square-foot structure was converted into a nightspot in 1981 and has a capacity of 6,000 people. The place once sold 16,000 bottles of beer during a Hank Williams Jr. show and features thirty-two bars, a massive dance floor, and a hall of handprints from performers past. There is no mechanical bull—damn liability insurance!—but there are live bull-riding performances on weekend nights. Its walls and ceilings clad in cowboy hats, the White Elephant Saloon (106 E. Exchange Ave., 817-624-8273, www.whiteelephantsaloon.com) is a one-of-a-kind vintage watering hole, pure Texas and pure West. The place takes its name from a legendary watering hole where guys like Bat Masterson and Wyatt Earp gambled that closed in 1916. When the stockyards were revitalized in 1976, the White Elephant was reborn as a raucous honky-tonk dance hall. Downtown, the Flying Saucer Draught Emporium (111 E. Fourth St., 817-336-7468, www.beerknurd.com) is the original in a chain with more than a dozen locations and a paradise for suds lovers, featuring seventy-seven taps and beers from all over the world. Located on Sundance Square, the Saucer is a good place to start or finish a night of escapades in the Fort.

Dallas Nightlife

Of all the gin joints in Dallas, I'm partial to Lee Harvey's (1807 Gould St., 214-428-1555, www.leeharveys.com), a worn-out old dive with a massive Austin-style yard. There's a kitchen and plenty of funky personality. Lee Harvey's is a bit out of the way south of downtown, pretty much by its lonesome in a questionable neighborhood where Dallas apparently got its start. You'll find your densest concentration of watering holes (and killer murals on the redbricks) in Deep Ellum: the graffiti-bedecked (even the beer mugs are Sharpied beyond recognition) hamburger joint/honky-tonk that is Adair's Saloon (2624 Commerce St., 214-939-9900, www.adairssaloon.com); Double Wide Bar (3510 Commerce St., 214-887-6510, www.double-wide.com), a rock venue modeled after a trailer, complete with a faux tornado on the roof; the artsy, indie-rock-oriented Club Dada (2720 Elm St., 214-742-3400, www.myspace.com/clubdada); and Sons of Hermann Hall (3414 Elm St., 214-747-4422, www.sonsofhermann.com), housed in a 1910 structure that once served as the meeting place for the Dallas chapter of a fraternal organization of the same name, now a rollicking honky-tonk open Wednesday through Saturday nights.

HUH?

Dallas, the Birthplace of the Church of the SubGenius
www.subgenius.com

First I printed out some pages off the Internet. Then I bought *The Book of the SubGenius*. Then *Revelation X*. Somewhere along the line, I realized this stuff wasn't a joke. These people were telling me the truth. We need more slack.

I discovered that J. R. "Bob" Dobbs was the key to my own happiness and my own maximization of slack. Dang it all if this stuff doesn't work. We all need more slack. Go to

STAR MAPS

- Archer City is best-selling author and Oscar-winning screenwriter Larry McMurtry's hometown, and it served as the location for many film adaptations of his books *The Last Picture Show* and *Texasville*. His antiquarian bookstore, Booked Up, is a bibliophile's dream (www.bookedupac.com) and spread across four buildings in downtown Archer City.

- Country legend Willie Nelson opened a music venue, Willie's Place (254-582-8433, www.biowillieusa.com), at the Carl's Corner truck stop off Interstate 35 south of Dallas in 2008.

- At the age of fifteen, Jerry Lee Lewis was sent to God's Institute Bible School in Waxahachie, but was promptly expelled.

- On TV's *Dallas*, J. R. Ewing plotted and connived from Southfork Ranch in Plano (www.southfork.com), now open to the public for tours and special events.

- Scarlett O'Hardy's *Gone with the Wind* Museum in Jefferson (www.scarlettohardy.com) features a *GWTW*-themed Christmas tree, books, dolls, and a reproduction of the green drapery dress Vivien Leigh wore in the film.

- *Munsters* superfans Sandra and Charles McKee transformed their place at 3636 Brown Street in Waxahachie into TV's 1313 Mockingbird Lane. The McKee's Munster Mansion (www.munstermansion.com) is only open to the public on Halloween, but visitors are welcome to take photos from the gates year-round.

- The Mary Kay Museum (www.marykay.com), at 16251 Dallas Parkway in Addison, covers the story of makeup tycoon Mary Kay Ash and her iconic Pink Cadillac.

Dallas, go to Austin, go anywhere—wherever you see the opportunity for the most slack.

The scant information available on the church's origins describes the first public church gatherings attracting sizeable crowds in Dallas in 1979, before the phenomenon spread beyond Texas's borders and *The Book of the SubGenius* first went to press in 1983. The Church of the SubGenius founder, Reverend Ivan Stang, made shadowy references to the church's Skyscraper HQ in Dallas, but—presumably in search of more slack—Stang moved to the Cleveland area in the late 1990s and continues to run the church from there.

Praise "Bob!"

Cockroach Hall of Fame & Museum
At the Pest Shop, 2231-B W. 15th St., Plano
972-519-0355
www.pestshop.com

Michael Bohdan launched his bug-killing business in the late 1980s on a shoestring. "I had no money to advertise," he says, "so I came up with an idea to pay $1,000 for Dallas's largest cockroach." Not only did he land an impressive American cockroach specimen, he also gained national notoriety after Johnny Carson brought him on *The Tonight Show* to discuss the contest. Bohdan brought a roach on a leash to walk on Carson's desk and immediately received a dozen calls to become a spokesman for pesticide companies and took a gig with Combat. Wearing his Cockroach Dundee hat, its brim adorned with the lacquered bodies of hissing cockroaches, he explained his duties, including judging the company's Best-Dressed Cockroach contest, which basically involved dioramas made with dead roaches and other materials. Bohdan now proudly displays a number of entries at his

Cockroach Hall of Fame & Museum, located in a strip mall in suburban Plano. The winner, The ComBates Motel, is there, as are Liberoachi, Sam Roach Kinison, Imelda Marcosroach, and Norman Roachwell. "People don't like bugs, but once they see them dressed up, they change their attitude," notes Bohdan. "It's funny how an insect that's been around for 350 million years can still get attention." However, preservation of these masterpieces can be an issue. "Cockroaches are so fragile when they die. If you don't touch them, they'll last." Sage advice indeed.

Salt Palace
100 W. Garland St., Grand Saline
903-962-5631

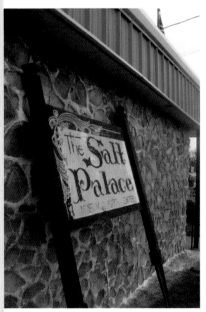

Grand Saline is named Grand Saline for a reason: the vast salt deposits here would season the country's food for the next 20 millennia or so. The Morton Salt Mine, south of town, has dug 750 feet into these deposits—only 19,250 feet to go. To honor the industry, Grand Saline's leaders built the first Salt Palace in 1936, fashioned after the Alamo. But salt structures do not do too well in the rain—"They melt away," says a local—so a second salt building went up in 1960. It also melted. In 1975, a third Salt Palace was built. It melted as well. Locals solved the problem in 1993 by creating a more permanent, non-salt structure to be re-salted annually for the big June event, the Salt Festival. Stop in the Salt Palace for a look at pictures of salt mines and the baskets of salt crystals: little ones are free, but a big hunk of salt will set you back $5.

Ezekiel Airship
Depot Museum
204 W. Marshall St., Pittsburg
903-856-0463
www.pittsburgtxmuseum.com

Inspired by the description of a flying machine in the biblical Book of Ezekiel that was propelled by spinning wheels and somehow made up of a man, a lion, an eagle, and an ox, Reverend Burrell Cannon first envisioned his airship in the 1880s. He started drafting sketches, building prototypes, and pitching his idea to investors. After he raised $20,000, Burrell built the real deal. In 1903—a year before the Wright Brothers' plane took flight at Kitty Hawk, North Carolina—Burrell's aptly named *Ezekiel Airship* allegedly flew a distance of 167 feet at a modest elevation of ten feet above the ground, but there is little in the way of proof. Soon after this supposed first flight, the vessel was destroyed in a windstorm. At first, Cannon considered the end of the *Ezekiel Airship* to be God's will, allegedly stating, "I want no more to do with it." Regardless, he returned to the aviation business soon thereafter, but he never again got an airship off the ground. Local mechanic Bob Loughery built a replica of Cannon's doomed airship in the 1980s. It now hangs from the rafters of the Depot Museum in Pittsburg and features plenty of spinning wheels, but no mutant man-lion-eagle-ox hybrid.

Aurora UFO Crash: The Original Roswell?
Aurora Cemetery
Cemetery Rd. south of TX Hwy. 114

In April 1897, a UFO allegedly crashed into a windmill in Aurora, killing its diminutive alien pilot. The extraterrestrial corpse was buried in the town's cemetery, but the grave has since been robbed. Military officials are rumored to have been involved. After UFO investigators found a rare chunk of aluminum-iron on the site in the 1990s, they pushed for the grave to be exhumed to check it for any alien DNA, but

Aurorans fought this tooth and nail. Skeptics, however, claim the whole thing was a hoax from the outset, a scheme to lure tourists after the railroad bypassed the town, perpetrated by locals to this day.

Lake Weatherford Monster
Weatherford

Described as a gargantuan hairless armadillo with glowing red eyes or a man-eating aquatic devil-cow with a bizarre mating call, the Lake Weatherford monster has been the subject of local legend for some time. There have been numerous sightings of the foul-smelling beast over the years, many of them involving heavy drinking by the monster-seers, but never has its existence been verified beyond a doubt. Of course, another local legend also holds that Abraham Lincoln faked his own death—à la Elvis Presley five score and a dozen years later—and lived out his years as Alexander "Billy Bob" Hamilton, an employee at a Weatherford feed store.

Texas Bigfoot
Sightings across East Texas
www.texasbigfoot.org

Not to be outdone by the big guy's higher profile in the Pacific Northwest, the podiatrically gifted but shy giant has been spotted tromping around the Piney Woods of East Texas for more than a century. In the 1830s, there was the Wild Woman of the Navidad, the Marion County Monster burst onto the scene in the 1960s, and the 1970s saw the emergence of the Hawley Him. Most sightings take place under the cover of night in the many swamps and bogs in and around Jefferson, Longview, and Commerce, although upright eight-footers have been reported as far east as Fort Worth. One of the best spots to see a Texas Bigfoot specimen in its natural environment is otherworldly, moss-draped Caddo Lake. There are a number of boatmen who give tours of the lake based out of the odd little town of Uncertain.

GRUB

The Origins of Dr Pepper

Dr Pepper Museum
300 S. 5th St., Waco
254-757-1025

Dublin Dr Pepper Museum

105 E. Elm St., Dublin
888-398-1024
www.dublindrpepper.com

Invented in 1885, Dr Pepper came to be when pharmacist Charles Alderton made a "suicide" out of all twenty-three flavors at Wade Morrison's soda fountain in Waco, and people couldn't get enough of the new drink and dubbed it the Waco. Morrison later renamed it to curry favor with a real Dr. Pepper, the father of a girl he was courting. Dr. Pepper was none too impressed and told Morrison to stay away from his daughter, but the name stuck. In 1891, Morrison sold the rights to Sam Houston Prim, who lived in the area near Dublin, and became the first bottler of Dr Pepper outside of Waco. In the ensuing years, Dr Pepper boomed to become one of the top three soft drinks in the country and the best-selling noncola drink. The 1960 Cuban embargo caused the prices of cane sugar to explode, and bottlers nationwide turned to cheaper, domestic high-fructose syrup instead. Dublin Dr Pepper is one of the few bottlers of soft drinks that stuck with sugar after prices exploded—thus the original Dr Pepper formula remains flowing at the Dublin bottler. Museums in both Waco and Dublin tell compelling stories of the early days of Dr Pepper and offer gift shops with everything from Dr Pepper lip balm and beef jerky to Dr Pepper marinade and cake mix. Soda lovers should also check out the Soda Gallery at 408 N. Bishop Avenue in Dallas's Oak Cliff neighborhood (214-946-7632, www.thesodagallery.com), a store that stocks nearly 200 sodas from all over the world.

Fruitcake Heaven: Collin Street Bakery

401 W. 7th Ave., Corsicana
903-874-7477 or 800-297-7400
www.collinstreet.com

The home of the DeLuxe Texas Fruitcake, Collin Street Bakery still uses the same recipe from master German baker Gus Weidmann that it did when it opened in 1896. The resulting pecan- and pineapple-heavy delicacy is a fruitcake for fruitcake connoisseurs. Fruitcakes and all sorts of other baked goods—including plenty of free samples—are available at the original location in downtown Corsicana, as well newer locations off Interstate 45 in Corsicana, and Interstate 35 in Waco.

Navarro Pecan Company

2131 Hwy. 31 E, Corsicana
903-872-1337
www.navarropecan.com

The Texas state nut is the pecan and the state tree is the native pecan. A stop at Navarro Pecan should suffice for filling the pecan needs of any visitor to the Lone Star State. One of the world's largest pecan-shelling facilities, the place shucks some 50 million pounds of nuts a year. The Pecan Producers International outlet store on-site offers free pecan samples and sells yogurt-dipped pecans, jalapeño pecans, cinnamon pecans, pecan pralines, and pecan rolls.

Athens: Birthplace of the Hamburger?

While Paris is northeast of Dallas, Athens lies to the southeast, and unlike its European-inspired counterpart, features
no scale replica of a landmark—there is no Acropolis with
a cowboy hat. Instead, Athens is where Uncle Fetch Davis
invented the hamburger in the 1880s. While other towns
across the country maintain to be the burger's birthplace
(see New Haven, Connecticut, Seymour, Wisconsin, and
Hamburg, New York), Athens cemented its claim with a
plaque on Davis's former eatery on the downtown square
that commemorates this culinary leap forward toward ever
faster and faster food. However, Davis left Athens in 1904,
never to return with his recipe, and headed to the St. Louis
World's Fair, where the hamburger's ascent to the top of the
country's food heap is well documented to have begun. The
best place in town to toast the birth of the hamburger with
a hamburger is the Old West Bean & Burger (1500 E. Tyler
St., 903-675-8100).

Mayhaws

Mayhaws are the swamp fruit that are harvested from the
lakes and bayous of East Texas every May and are a favorite
fruit for jellymakers. The citrus-sweet jelly is usually $7 a
jar, but the fruit can be found for free floating in big clumps
in the wetlands, if you know where to look. Mayhaws are
edible but not altogether tasty straight off the tree, and they
are often used to make syrup, juice, and wine, as well as the
popular jelly.

JFK: HISTORY, TRAGEDY, CONSPIRACY

FIVE DAYS, 200 MILES, COUNTLESS THEORIES

It's Martin Luther King Jr. Day 2009. Tomorrow Barack Obama will be sworn in as the country's forty-third president.

I'm driving around a somewhat bedraggled black neighborhood east of Dallas, listening to NPR. Terry Gross is interviewing Ta-Nehisi Coates about Martin Luther King Jr. and his steadfast push for civil rights.

"Of course, he paid for it with his life," Coates says, "and we're all fearful for Barack Obama."

The next subject is an angrier black man, a reverend who says that King's nonviolent, politically active worldview had been replaced by crack, hip-hop, BET, and cultural isolation. Forty years after his death, 90 percent of kids in the south Bronx don't even know who King is, he adds. "It's more segregated than ever."

Up ahead, a barricade and police cars with flashing red and blues block the road for a MLK Day parade on MLK Boulevard. I park under an overpass and walk up to the intersection.

A marching band passes, followed by a truck bearing a portrait of Dr. King and a dozen Expose the 9/11 Cover-Up placards. A grinning graybeard, one of the few Caucasians besides me, walks along the sidewalk and hands me a free newspaper, *The Truth Times: The Truth They Won't Tell You.*

A couple of the headlines read: Were Explosives Used on 9/11? and Who Did It? FBI says, 'No hard evidence connecting Bin Laden to 9/11.'

There are few details on who plotted the alleged bombings. Apparently, the BBC was in on it—they reported the collapse of building seven a full twenty minutes early—conspiring with Larry Silverstein in concocting massive corporate fraud.

The parade continues, more cars than floats, a few ATVs and Harleys and hot rods, plenty of Obama shirts and hats and chants, kids eating candy, but very few white faces in the crowd, a seemingly segregated event.

"Got a light?" a guy asks.

"Excuse me, sir," a little girl says as I tell him no. She hands me a postcard from a local salon that shows a trio of black women with slick hairdos, "where you can become a star."

After a half hour, the parade is petering out, and I return to my car under the overpass and drive through Fair Park, passing a black woman in white face and a Rastafarian float before heading through a tunnel on the east side of the park. A cluster of weathered shacks sits on the other side. An old black man sits on his porch. I slowly drive by and give him a nod. He doesn't nod back. Maybe he doesn't see me.

Soon I'm walking the streets below the gleaming spires of

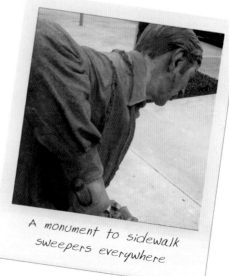

A monument to sidewalk sweepers everywhere

downtown Dallas. A rhythmic pounding of heavy equipment emanates from a nearby tower that's under construction. There are few people walking the sidewalks, but many more driving the streets. (One of them nearly runs me over.)

A Styrofoam cup bounces down the street, its march punctuated by hollow thuds. Past a crowded bus stop, a whirlwind of garbage swirls around an empty parking lot.

I zig across Founders Plaza to John F. Kennedy Memorial Plaza, centered on a white enclosure around a black block labeled John Fitzgerald Kennedy. An Arabic couple chats near the monument, their kids playing in the grass.

I start to read the plaque on the sidewalk in front of the plaza and notice that someone has slathered some sort of goo all over JFK's face—maybe fast-food gravy, well, *hopefully* fast-food gravy. I can't help but scrape it off with some small leaves, the only available napkin substitute. Nasty. I need to find a sink to wash my hands.

I make my way toward the Sixth Floor Museum, up just a couple of blocks on the north side of Dealey Plaza. Currently a museum, the sixth floor of the former book depository is where Lee Harvey Oswald allegedly shot John F. Kennedy on November 22, 1963.

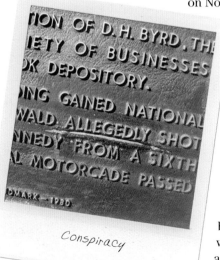

Conspiracy

On the corner across from the building, a bespectacled man with shaggy brown hair is selling newspapers that detail the events of that awful day, as well as the various conspiracy theories surrounding the assassination.

"How much?" I ask.

"Five bucks," he answers, revealing a missing front tooth.

I decline, but the light turns before I can cross the street. "So what theory do you believe?" I ask the paper peddler.

"Oswald didn't do it. It wasn't even Oswald's gun that killed him."

"Then who did it?"

He leers at me and answers, "People in the government. People in power. They wanted to get rid of him. They made it look like the Mafia did it."

I start to ask him if Jack Ruby was working with the Mafia or the government and realize it's probably not the best idea. I've got shit to do.

I make my way into the museum, but realize I don't have enough time for a tour—there is only about an hour left on my parking meter across downtown. Out front, the historical plaque features a prominent man-made scratch under the word *allegedly* between "Lee Harvey Oswald" and "shot John F. Kennedy."

Next I stroll over to the grassy knoll, the alleged site of the alleged sniper allegedly responsible for one very real, very catastrophic head wound.

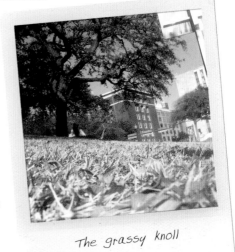

The grassy knoll

A Segway tour group arrives. People from all over the world wander up and down the sidewalk, pointing and talking, rubbing their chins, taking photos of the book depository, the street where the motorcade passed four decades before, the grassy knoll, empty shots of horrible and invisible past events. There is something macabre about this particular tourist attraction.

A lanky fellow in a Cowboys cap talks to a European-looking couple in low tones, detailing his four-shooter theory. Flintlike chirps drift down from the boughs above. A plastic-sheathed poster board features the eight still-frames from the Zapruder film where the blurry president collapses into his wife's lap.

Heading back east toward my car, I stop at a cafe for a cup of coffee and check my e-mail and the top CNN.com headlines. One catches my eye: Men in black on alert for snipers. I click it and read the story on the Secret Service's elite squad of countersnipers who work most any public presidential event, as they will at Obama's inauguration tomorrow.

A half hour later, I'm plopping my bags down on the floor of my room in the Westin City Center. I finally wash my hands of the remnants of the alleged gravy.

My next move, a few hours later, is to Deep Ellum, just east of downtown. Loaded with tattoo parlors and watering holes, but still relatively sturdy and clean, the funky and historic neighborhood seems on the verge of gentrification (plenty of new lofts) and it's clearly a weekend destination (reams of parking lots). But there are no people on the streets on this Monday in January.

But there are a few in the bars. After a Shiner in a graffiti-streaked mug at Adair's Saloon, a graffiti-clad honky-tonk, I succumb to hunger and eat a cheeseburger and a side of fries. After another Shiner, I wander the neighborhood and check out a few more bars.

Deep Ellum artwork

Then I work my way back west and head south over the highway.

There are people at the bus stops. A lone kid paces the sidewalk on the other side of the street. A shadowy black cat from a distance becomes a crumpled black trash bag up close.

I make my way to a stinky vintage dive, Lee Harvey's, with a big yard out front, and take a seat at the bar. There are old beer signs on the walls, including a Schlitz. A fake log glows red in the fireplace.

The bar features well-worn islands in the Formica where countless beers have rested. An image of Kennedy's bloody head flashes through my mind.

I write some notes on a pad as I drink a beer. So does the guy three bar stools to my left.

"We'll have a new president tomorrow," says the bartender.

I'll drink to that.

· · · · ·

Waking up at 8 AM, I flip the tube back on. Obama is in church.

"It's a celebration," says one commentator.

"There's a sense of a new day," adds another.

Apparently, Vice President Andrew Johnson was drunk at Lincoln's second inauguration, and John Adams was angrily absent from that of Thomas Jefferson, his successor. Andrew Jackson's inauguration snowballed into a rowdy White House party.

Obama goes in to have coffee with Bush.

"This is a step in our history, not just an inauguration."

It's hard to separate whether the people are celebrating Obama's arrival or Bush's departure or both.

The political stars begin to arrive.

I somehow end up on the Wikipedia page covering Lincoln's assassination, then click through to the link of all US presidential assassination attempts: four successful (Lincoln, Kennedy, McKinley, and Garfield—although Garfield died eleven weeks later due to infections brought on because of substandard medical care), about twenty unsuccessful, including some pretty far-fetched ones. Some people believe Warren Harding and Zachary Taylor were poisoned.

The strangest conspiracy might be that of McKinley's ghost and New York barman John Schrank, who shot Theodore Roosevelt when he was running for a third term as a Progressive in 1912, four years after he left office. A fifty-page speech in Teddy's breast pocket apparently slowed the bullet just enough so it did not pierce his lung, so he of course croaked through the speech before seeking medical attention. He elected to keep the bullet in his chest rather than have it surgically removed because a botched surgical removal contributed to McKinley's death after he was shot by anarchist Leon Czolgosz in 1901. Schrank claimed that McKinley's ghost told him to take out Roosevelt as a warning to third termers everywhere and spent the rest of his life in a mental institution in Wisconsin.

Bush's motorcade heads up Pennsylvania Avenue. "In exactly one hour," says Wolf Blitzer, "Barack Obama becomes president of the United States." My pulse quickens.

After First Lady of Soul Aretha Franklin, the Obama girls enter, then other very important people. Finally, Dubya appears on the TV, biting his lip, smirking.

Anderson Cooper points out that the Capitol Building and the White House were built on the backs of slaves.

Bush emerges to fanfare and shakes a bunch of hands. They wheel out Cheney, looking very much like the villainous Mr. Potter in *It's a Wonderful Life*. There is a smattering of boos.

I can't help but be nervous. There is something eerie about the words "the Lincoln Bible," I think. But Obama, as usual, looks calm.

"Barack H. Obama" is announced to the crowd—that might be the first time I've heard it with an *H*—then Dianne Feinstein speaks, Rick Warren prays, Aretha Franklin sings, and Biden is sworn in on a ridiculously large Bible. Unlike the Martin Luther King parade the day before, the crowd at the inauguration looks remarkably integrated.

As Yo-Yo Ma and Itzhak Perlman play, Blitzer interjects, "It's 12:01 Eastern. Even though he has not been administered the oath of office, Barack Obama is now the president of the United States."

I eye a man in a fedora behind a chain-link fence with suspicion. It's probably the fence.

During the oath Obama finally appears nervous, stumbling over a few lines. I'm definitely not a big fan of the subsequent twenty-one-gun salute. Gunshots always sound bad to me, regardless of their context.

"Forty-four Americans have now taken the presidential oath," Obama begins his inaugural address. His calm and collected aura returns and gathers steam as the speech goes on.

Of critics of his ambitious plans, he says, "Their memories are short. For they have forgotten what this great nation has already done." He's referring to the good things the nation has done, of course, but I can't help but be reminded of some of the country's collective bad deeds, namely slavery and assassinations.

He repeatedly stresses that this is the beginning of a new, post-Bush era, with lines like "We are ready to lead once more" and "The world has changed, and we must change with it."

The speech ends and the crowd cheers. Dubya claps and smirks to Obama's left. Please leave already, sir.

In the CNN aftermath, I learn Chief Justice John Roberts messed up the oath, leading to Obama's apparent verbal stumble. I can hear the conspiracy theorists now.

My nervousness fades, but I remain wary and a bit overwhelmed by the enormity of the country's problems.

After Blitzer says Obama's "penmanship is really excellent," I know it's time to leave my room. Outside, a blast of wintry air surprises me. Grabbing a sandwich on the way, I make it over to Dealey Plaza and the Sixth Floor Museum.

The paper peddlers are still out in full force. I enter the ground floor, get a ticket and the audio tour headphones, and take the elevator alone to the sixth floor of the former Texas School Book Depository.

I'm struck by the similarity between the rhetoric of Kennedy and Obama, each speaking about moving forward into a new era, and the similarity between the rhetoric of both men's detractors.

The thirty-fifth president also brought youth and style to the White House, and he brought the first little kids into the place in fifty years. He catalyzed the space program and started the Peace Corps and the National Endowment for the Arts, but his legislative thrusts were largely parried. There are displays on his roles in the Civil Rights Act and the Cuban Missile Crisis.

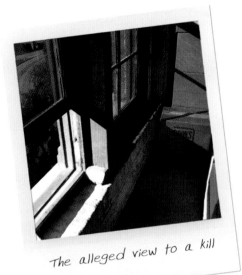

The alleged view to a kill

But the displays' focus quickly shifts to JFK's November 1963 trip to Texas to drum up political support for his looming 1964 campaign, diving into "a real political tempest," according to an old newsreel. There were concerns about right-wing extremists who had distributed flyers and placed a full-page ad in *The Dallas Morning News*, the former calling Kennedy a traitor, the latter claiming Dallas was a bastion of free-enterprise conservatism and Kennedy was a Communist sympathizer.

After landing at Love Field, Kennedy's motorcade begins its horrible crawl through downtown. "Fears were unjustified," says a commentator on the video. "There has been an overwhelming welcome for the president."

Soon another voice crackles from the past. "God, let it be a firecracker!"

The dark reality of the museum's story becomes clear. My eyes get teary. I'm not the only one. The details of the drive to the hospital and the subsequent lost medical cause are harrowing. This leads me to the window where Lee Harvey Oswald allegedly shot the president.

After he was apprehended, "He didn't act like an individual who'd just killed a police officer and certainly not one that had just shot the president of the United States," says an arresting officer.

Oswald died at the same hospital as JFK, just two days and seven minutes later, an hour after Mafia-connected, strip-club owner Jack Ruby walked into the city jail and shot him in the gut. Ruby died of cancer in prison four years later.

The United States' first presidential assassination since 1901 shocked the world. The somber funeral footage again primes the tear ducts. There's that damn twenty-one-gun salute. A woman in the museum blows her nose.

The next display details the ensuing investigations—the Warren Commission said Oswald acted alone, the House deemed it almost certainly a plot in the late 1970s, and the Justice Department closed the case in 1988. Next up are the many conspiracy theories, involving some combination of the CIA, the Mafia, Castro, the KGB, Texas oilmen, right-wing radicals, and an Oswald look-alike. And the fact that scores of material witnesses died.

A 1964 quote from Harrison Salisbury of *The New York Times* sums it up: "The year 2000 will see men still arguing about the president's death."

Polls in the 1960s showed just over half of the public thought Lee Harvey Oswald acted alone. By the 1980s, that figure rose to 80 percent.

There is a guest book near the exit. "We again have another young visionary president," begins one note from a Georgia woman who grew up in a Baptist family that taught her the killing of a Catholic "wasn't anything to be too upset about." She knew better now. Several other notes in the book link JFK and Obama.

In the gift shop, there are JFK T-shirts and JFK magnets, miniature busts, books, DVDs, JFK and Jackie dolls, and commemorative newspaper reprints.

Outside, a guy in a jogging suit named Jimmy is leafing through a magazine with graphic images, pointing out the different points on the street, the neck shot, the head shot. The motorcade route was changed the morning of the assassination, he adds. He tries to sell me a glossy magazine for $10. I decline and ask him who did it. He tells me there were four or five shooters, and Oswald wasn't one of them. He flips to a photo that shows a man who could be Oswald outside on the sidewalk as the motorcade passed the book depository.

"They had to blame someone," he says. He flips to another page and says, "They picked up these three guys acting like hobos over there," pointing to the nearby railroad tracks. One of them was Woody Harrelson's father, who did hits for the mob.

I walk over to investigate the storm drain above the grassy knoll, an alleged escape route. I see the lanky guy from yesterday in the Cowboys hat talking to three guys in polo shirts and listen in on the conversation.

"This is my twenty-third year of working here," he says. "I'm on my lunch break, but I could give you some basics."

He says a piece of skull was found by the central flagpole, an impossible angle for a shot fired from the sixth floor of the book depository. "It defies physics, the way I was brought up."

A witness saw Oswald in the second-floor lunchroom just before the motorcade passed, the lanky guy continues. Oswald would have had to be the world's best marksman and an Olympic runner to pull it off alone. "I call it like I see it," he says with a Texas drawl. He asks us four who we thought did it. The other three agree it was the CIA. I tell him I don't know.

"You want my opinion?" After implicating LBJ, the Russians, the Secret Service, and the Mafia, he tells a joke about a guy who dies and goes to Heaven and asks God who killed JFK. "Well, I've got a theory about that myself," answers God.

This guy doesn't seem to know either.

He finishes by saying, "You don't have to tip me, but…" The guys in the polo shirts slip him a twenty, putting me on the spot. I give him three singles, tell him I'm writing a book, and ask for his name.

"Sherman Hopkins."

"How'd you get your start here?"

"Well, a guy offered me a job in Dallas and…" He abruptly walks off and grabs three conspiracy papers from the nearest peddler—Sherman is clearly a ringleader—and tries to sell them to the guys who gave him the twenty. Before I know it, he's purposefully striding away from me across the plaza, too far ahead to follow.

I get back to my room for the tail end of Obama's inaugural parade and news that the Dow has sunk more than 300 points.

The historic moment is past. CNN gets back to having too much time on its hands. Wolf Blitzer says that the Ohio State University marching band is the largest brass and percussion ensemble in the world.

I call my high school friend Bobby, who lives in the north suburbs. A recent transplant to the area, he's never been to the Sixth Floor Museum.

"It doesn't seem like Oswald acted alone," I tell him.

"Did you hear about the conspiracy theory of Mike Shanahan coming to coach the Cowboys?" he retorts.

We coordinate meeting for dinner the next night. The Obamas hit the first of many inaugural balls. "First of all, how good looking is my wife?" he asks the crowd before the first dance. I head out for dinner.

But unlike the Obamas, I have no one to please. I slump onto a bar stool at the Angry Dog Pub, eat some nachos, drink some Shiners, and head back to my room at the hotel before 10 PM, just as the Obamas make it to the fourth of ten balls.

"This is a great moment for American fashion," says a fashion pundit on the TV.

The Obama girls apparently are up late with friends.

I smoke a little weed and plop onto the bed.

Was Oswald a patsy? Was it the vast right-wing conspiracy, backed by the Vatican and the Dallas police, fronted by a renegade CIA agent who was surgically altered to look just like Oswald?

Oswald defected to the USSR in 1959 at age nineteen and returned to the US three years later, a year and a half before November 22, 1963. Three things stand out in favor of his guilt: he said, "It's all over now," before wrestling with police in the Texas Theater; his stories to police were inconsistent—but the Dallas cops were in charge of the investigation and could have been in on it; and witnesses said they saw Oswald running around, brandishing a gun.

He was exhumed in 1981 in an effort to prove a look-alike did not take his place. His coffin was ruptured and his body was in pretty bad shape, but dental records showed it was indeed Oswald.

· · · · ·

The next morning, I still have Lee Harvey Oswald on my mind. He was dead forty-eight hours after the cops caught up with him at the Texas Theater in the Oak Cliff neighborhood, a few miles southwest of Dealey Plaza and seven blocks from his apartment. Jack Ruby just walked in and shot him. A whole armada of cops and none of them stopped him. And that was that.

"It's just too fucking perfect," I say to myself.

On the way to my car, I pass a granite-clad alcove fronted by a sign, Defense Contractors South, Annual Shareholders Meeting.

After defusing a conspiracy to charge me for three days of parking when my car was there for only two, I drive south of the city to see some sights. An economist on the radio, David Cay Johnston, says that the result of wealth redistribution through taxation is not trickle-down, and never has been, but in fact "Niagara-up."

"We have to stop thinking as if the world is coming to an end and everything is about us today," he says. "We need to start thinking about America and its freedoms enduring."

I eat a cheeseburger in Athens, the birthplace of the hamburger, where the local Republican Party still has a sign in its window touting, We Support Our President and

Our Troops. I wonder if it will stay up now that Bush is back in Texas.

Looping up to Dallas's north suburbs by 5 PM—taking note that this is likely the only metro area with streets named after both George H. W. Bush and Malcolm X—I meet my college friends Troy and Michelle and their nearly two-year-old daughter, Evelyn, for fried chicken at Babe's in Carrollton. My high-school friends Bobby and Kendra meet us there.

The deer head on the wall talks and the waitresses do the hokey-pokey and the fried chicken is excellent. I try to steer the conversation toward JFK, but get little response.

"I gotta be honest, I cringe every time Obama is in public," says Troy. "There's gotta be so many crazy racists who are just incensed that we have a black president."

Kendra offers another Dallas enigma: "Everybody that falls out of a boat here seems to drown."

But most of our conversations revolve around high school and college hijinks, as well as fried chicken and life in suburban Dallas. I crash on Troy and Michelle's spare bed and get a fairly early start on my next day. "Bye-bye," says Evy. "Bye-bye."

My first stop is the Oak Cliff neighborhood. After navigating the unseemly ring that surrounds the man-made jewel of downtown, passing a 7-11 surrounded by hordes of Latino day laborers and a few boutiques and art galleries, I park my car near the Texas Theater, where Oswald was apprehended. The theater was shuttered in 1989, restored in 2003, and is now open for special events. There is nothing on the marquee today.

It's 10:12 AM. It takes me about fifteen minutes to walk to Oswald's former boardinghouse, a route he was said to have dashed after changing his clothes at this apartment, shooting Dallas police officer Aaron Tippit.

On the way back to my car, I stop at another former Oswald residence on West Neely Street. It's a sunny blue-sky day. Birds chirp up and down the dilapidated block.

I stop at the Dallas Museum of Art and the Nasher Sculpture Center, then swing by Deep Ellum to take some sun-drenched photos of the mural-clad brick walls, before driving a half hour east to downtown Fort Worth and checking into the Holiday Inn Express & Suites in the late afternoon.

Just before sunset, I venture out on foot, passing a Masonic temple, its lawn alive with blackbirds. After circling Sundance Square in the heart of downtown, I settle on a bar stool at the Flying Saucer and order a local Rahr and Sons Blind Salamander Pale Ale. It's happy hour, so it's big.

A portly guy with salt-and-pepper hair takes the bar stool next to me. We strike up a conversation and he tells me he's betting on the Arizona Cardinals to cover the spread in the Super Bowl. "If you take the money line, you can bet $100 and make $225."

His name is Kojak, and he's the general manager of a local RV dealership.

Of course, I ask him who killed Kennedy.

It turns out he wrote a college paper on the subject. "I'm not 100 percent convinced it was Oswald," he says, espousing a theory that the true killer shot from the sewer drain.

Who did it then?

"Johnson had to be involved," says Kojak, also fingering the Mafia. "Just like UFOs, they don't believe the public can handle the truth. I was born Catholic. If there's an alien who came down and used the earth as a petri dish, and there's no God, and we knew the truth, it would ruin the Christian belief system and it would be like the stock market crash."

He tells me the RV business is pretty bad. "Obama's not helping much," he says. "Half of it is psychological."

Onward, Upward

Kojak tells me he'll buy me dinner at Del Frisco's Double Eagle Steak House, a swank joint a few blocks away. I take him up on it. We take his Jaguar—he valets it.

I find out he was in the restaurant business, but had to shut his place down because of gambling issues. "Now I'm looking at putting a place in Dubai. It's going to open in 2012."

"That's when the world's going to end," I say, "at least according to the Mayan calendar."

"That's right," says Kojak.

We split an order of shrimp rémoulade, a huge longbone steak, gourmet mac and cheese, and drink several Crown Royal and 7-Ups. After a while, Kojak begins trying to sell the restaurant some bottles from his $30,000 wine cellar. We have some sort of booze–ice cream concoction for dessert.

I end up getting completely smashed.

Later, I'm talking to the night desk clerk, slurring, rambling about JFK.

"What do Kennedy and Obama have in common?" he asks with a grin.

I shake my head.

"Nothing yet."

Horrible joke. I'm too drunk to tell him off.

· · · · ·

Hungover and groggy, I eat a big breakfast in hopes of soaking up the excess Crown Royal in my gut before heading out for my day. I check out the cultural district, drop in the Modern Art Museum-Fort Worth and the National Cowgirl Museum & Hall of Fame.

By midafternoon, I'm driving past a horde of homeless people on East Lancaster Avenue. A few minutes later, I'm parking my car at Shannon Rose Hill Cemetery, where they buried Lee Harvey Oswald two days after JFK's murder.

The sun tucked behind a wispy layer of clouds, it takes me a good half-hour of wandering around the graveyard to find Oswald's marker. I think that I'm more confused about JFK's assassination than I was before the trip.

I finally do find Lee Harvey's marker, take a picture, and gaze at the simple slab. It reads *Oswald*—no other words, no dates, nearly anonymous amidst the rows. The discovery does nothing to illuminate whether he was a lone wacko or a patsy.

Guilty or not, murder is an awful crime, a terrible thing, the worst of humanity.

Where to go...

John F. Kennedy Memorial Plaza
Main and Commerce Sts., Dallas

The Sixth Floor Museum
411 Elm St., Dallas
214-747-6660
www.jfk.org

Adair's Saloon
2624 Commerce St., Dallas
214-939-9900
www.adairssaloon.com

Lee Harvey's
1807 Gould St., Dallas
214-428-1555
www.leeharveys.com

Angry Dog Pub
2726 Commerce St., Dallas
214-741-4406
www.angrydog.com

Babe's
1006 W. Main St., Carrollton
972-245-7773
www.babeschicken.com

Texas Theater
231 W. Jefferson Blvd., Dallas
www.oakclifffoundation.org

Dallas Museum of Art
1717 N. Harwood St., Dallas
214-922-1200
www.dallasmuseumofart.org

Nasher Sculpture Center
2001 Flora St., Dallas
214-242-5100
www.nashersculpturecenter.org

Flying Saucer Draught Emporium
111 E. Fourth St., Fort Worth
817-336-7468
www.beerknurd.com

Del Frisco's Double Eagle Steak House
812 Main St., Fort Worth
817-877-3999
www.delfriscos.com

Modern Art Museum-Fort Worth
3200 Darnell St., Fort Worth
817-738-9215
www.themodern.org

National Cowgirl Museum & Hall of Fame
1720 Gendy St., Fort Worth
817-336-4475
www.cowgirl.net

Lee Harvey Oswald's Grave
Shannon Rose Hill
Memorial Park
7301 E. Lancaster Ave.,
Fort Worth

SAN ANTONIO AND SOUTH TEXAS

INTRODUCTION

The heart of Texas history, the spot where a lone spark blew up into a proudly fiery star, is preserved like a bug in amber.

But the Alamo's modern urban surroundings now include a wax museum (its inhabitants would have surely been melted by Santa Anna's army if they had been hanging around in 1835) and a 3-D thrill ride, not to mention the gift shop inside the former Spanish mission's walls, where the state now stations a full-time Texas Ranger, primarily to keep travel writers from photographing the Alamo snow globes.

But beyond the Alamo's historical presence in a sky-scraping downtown, the city is often criticized as a bit sedate. A bit too sedate, perhaps. Keep San Antonio Lame, reads a sticker parodying the Keep Austin Weird campaign. But the near-tropical climate and the laid-back vibe make being lame pretty comfortable. And this is nothing if not a friendly city—even the bums have good manners.

Broadly, San Antonio resembles some combination of a major American city, Disneyland, and a major Mexican city.

But no matter what, do not drink the water in the River Walk, no matter your country of origin.

South of San Antonio is a vast, sparsely settled plain, furry with trees and cacti and a particularly fertile spot for fruits and vegetables and rattlesnakes and raccoons. If you're keeping score, the raccoons appear to be losing to the cars.

Farther south, on the great green snake of an international border that is the Rio Grande, Laredo, trying to distance itself from its unruly sister city Nuevo Laredo, remains the best place in the West to get a $15 embroidered Western shirt, and the McAllen-Brownsville metroplex in the Lower Rio Grande Valley, booming with both people and alligators, is the best place for $10 suitcases and $1 sunglasses.

STATS & FACTS

- The trademark arch on the Alamo's facade was added by the United States Army in 1850, fourteen years after the infamous battle took place here.

- Laredo is the largest inland port in the United States.

- Nine-banded armadillos were first spotted crossing the river into Texas in the vicinity of Rio Grande City in 1849. Their march to Dallas took about a century, but they've since become roadkill as far east as Georgia and Florida.

- Texas is typically the second biggest pecan-producing state (after Georgia), averaging about 60 million pounds a year.

Cross the Rio Grande, and you're in Mexico. Might as well have a cerveza or *tres* now that you're here.

BIG THINGS AND OTHER ROAD ART

Popeye Statues
Two locations in downtown Crystal City

The Spinach Capital of the World obviously needs a fitting mascot, and who better than that foulmouthed, one-eyed, pipe-toking sailor man? Well, two foulmouthed, one-eyed, pipe-toking sailor men, of course. Crystal City's town center sports a pair of Popeye statues, one from 1937 and another from 2007, and both of them are fully functional spinach pitchmen, complete with spindly biceps and meaty forearms.

World's Largest Rattlesnake
154 TX Hwy. 44, Freer

This ready-to-strike replica reptilian is located in the home of the annual Freer Rattlesnake Roundup, an annual festival that began in the 1960s. The event is also dubbed a world's largest, but the folks behind the rattlesnake roundup in Sweetwater, Texas, will argue with you on that point. Critics say both events—which involve the stomping, decapitation, and immolation of many snakes—are inhumane. I agree, but the statue still is okay in my book.

World's Largest Killer Bee
311 S. 3rd St., Hidalgo

You'd think you'd want to keep a lid on any and all references to Hidalgo's status as the killer-bee capital of the country— the city is near the site where Africanized honeybees were

Read:

- *The Gates of the Alamo by Stephen Harrigan*
- *On the Border: Portraits of America's Southwestern Frontier by Tom Miller*
- *O. Henry's Texas Stories by O. Henry*
- *A Land So Strange: The Epic Journey of Cabeza de Vaca by Andrés Résendez*

Listen:

- *El Corazón by Steve Earle*
- *Locust Abortion Technician by the Butthole Surfers*
- *Before the Next Teardrop Falls by Freddy Fender*

Watch:

- *The Alamo (the one with John Wayne)*
- *The Alamo (the one with Billy Bob Thornton)*
- *Pee-wee's Big Adventure (the one with Pee-wee Herman)*

To-Do Checklist:

- *Visit the Alamo*
- *Take pictures of the Alamo*
- *Remember the Alamo*

first spotted in the United States in 1990—but former Hidalgo mayor John Franz instead promoted the distinction by raising $20,000 to build an eye-grabbing, twenty-foot-long killer bee next to city hall.

Big Strawberries
Poteet

While not in the same league as the water-tower strawberry across town, the 1,600-pound berry in front of the Poteet Volunteer Fire Department is perhaps the world's largest strawberry that is not a water tower. Both big pieces of fruit celebrate Poteet as Texas's strawberry capital, producing nearly half of the state's fruit.

Watermelon Statue
Main St., Dilley

While not the world's largest by any means, a sizable watermelon missing a sizable chunk lays Dilley's claim to the coveted title of Watermelon Capital of Texas. Its primary rivals are Luling, featuring a watermelon water tower and the annual Watermelon Thump festival (www.watermelonthump.com), Knox City, and Hempstead.

Oil-Pump Art
All over Luling

Not just anybody looks at an oil pump and sees a canvas. But somebody in Luling evidently did just that—200 times. There are oil pumps done up like kids on a seesaw, a cow jumping over the moon, a quarterback throwing a football, and, inexplicably, a flamingo driving a car.

World's Second-Largest Pecan
At the Guadalupe County Courthouse
101 E. Court St., Seguin

Measuring just over five feet from end to end, the oversized pecan on the courthouse lawn in Seguin is dedicated to Cabeza de Vaca, the legendary Spanish explorer who first took note of the native nut on the Guadalupe River when he was imprisoned by the natives in the Seguin area in the mid-fifteenth century. Sadly, a considerably larger pecan in Missouri has outdone this specimen as the world's largest, but it still stands as a half-ton concrete monument to the county's pecan industry.

R.I.P.

John Nance Garner IV (a.k.a. Cactus Jack), 1868–1967
Uvalde Cemetery
US 90, Uvalde

The vice president, who described the office of the vice presidency as "not worth a bucket of warm piss" (often censored to "warm spit," an editorialization John Nance Garner described as being "pantywaist"), and Speaker of the House didn't mince words. Garner earned his Cactus Jack nickname from his losing effort pushing the prickly pear cactus for Texas State Flower (the bluebonnet of course won out) and kept it by making his mark as a prickly, outspoken politician.

VICE

La Tuna
100 Probandt St., San Antonio
210-212-5727
www.latunagrill.com

Just about as perfect as a watering hole gets, this bar just on the other side of the railroad tracks south of downtown San Antonio consists of several structures built of wood and corrugated metal, including a bar and a restaurant. Both are killer. Grab some grub and head to the bar—behind which a Pee-wee doll rides a mounted tuna—or the spacious outdoors, complete with a stage, dozens of picnic tables, and gravel consisting primarily of flattened bottle caps.

Peyoteros
Between Rio Grande City and Laredo

The only legal peyote dealers in the United States—all three of them—are in South Texas. The growing range of the hallucinogenic cactus extends from northern Mexico into the Rio Grande Valley and the Big Bend region. A few licensed peyoteros in South Texas harvest the buttons and sell them to religious users. The practice has been a way of life in these parts since the nineteenth century.

Spoetzl Brewery
603 E. Brewery St., Shiner
361-594-2294
www.shiner.com

This is it, the oldest brewery in Texas and home of what may as well be the official state beer, Shiner Bock. Founded in 1909, the brewery was soon taken over by its namesake in Kosmos Spoetzl, a German brewmaster who relocated to rural Texas after stints making suds in Cairo and Canada, bringing with him the old family recipe that is Shiner Bock. A modest brewery down a two-lane highway, Spoetzl is surprisingly generous with its samples, granting visitors four complimentary seven-ounce samples per visit. There are plenty of non-Bock Shiners, like Shiner Blonde and Shiner Black and Shiner Light, as well as plenty of schwag: Shiner T-shirts, Shiner sweatbands, Shiner umbrellas, Shiner inflatables, and pretty much Shiner everything else. Tours are available on weekdays at 11 AM and 1:30 PM.

STAR MAPS

- Dick Cheney shot his friend Harry Whittington in the face at the private Armstrong Ranch, between Harlingen and Kingsville.

- While wearing a dress, heavy-metal superstar Ozzy Osbourne was infamously arrested after pissing on the Alamo in 1982. He was subsequently banned from San Antonio for a full decade.

- Just west of San Antonio in Helotes, Floore's Country Store (www.liveatfloores.com) was the center of the Texas country movement in the 1960s and 1970s and remains one of the most raucous honky-tonks in the Lone Star State.

- Simon Vega is the proprietor of a museum at his home called Little Graceland (701 W. Ocean Blvd., Los Fresnos, north of Brownsville, 956-233-5482, call for an appointment, www.littlegraceland.com). A former army buddy of Elvis Presley, Vega has dedicated half of his home to his museum of Elvis collectibles: dolls, plates, records—including every one of the King's sixty-four albums—newspaper clippings, old photos, even a spare medal Elvis received for good conduct. Explains Vega: "He got three and I got one. He gave me the extra."

  After they got back from Germany, Elvis offered Vega a job as a roadie, but instead he went back to his wife in South Texas and collected Elvis memorabilia through the years. "My wife ran me out of the house."

  Vega wrote a song about Elvis after his death in 1977, and he has a CD with a recording. The lyrics tout Elvis as "the greatest King," later adding, "All your movies were fantastic." I'm with you on the greatest King part, but I'm not too sure about the movies, Simon.

HUH?

Toilet Seat Museum

239 Abiso Ave., Alamo Heights
(just north of San Antonio)
210-824-7791
call in advance for an appointment

Retired plumber Barney Smith is without a doubt the world's foremost toilet-seat artist. On my visit, his garage-turned-museum showcased 855—and counting!—of his masterworks. In the late 1960s, Smith looked at a toilet seat and somehow saw a canvas. Now he's got a garage full of toilet seats decorated with everything from *Star Wars* action figures to arrowheads. Many seats are dedicated to media outlets that featured the museum; others have religious themes, and others still are

dedicated to the routes of various vacations Smith's taken over the years. His first features the horns of a buck; his personal favorite features Rudyard Kipling's poem "When Earth's Last Picture is Painted." And you can buy Smith's handmade souvenir magnets shaped like toilet seats.

Buckhorn Saloon and Museum
318 E. Houston St., San Antonio
210-247-4000
www.buckhornmuseum.com

If you've never gotten a gander at a mounted deer head with a bad case of barnacle buck, then this place is a must-stop. If you have, it's probably going to be old hat. Unless of course, like me, you take advantage of every opportunity to see a stuffed, two-headed calf. This is not to mention the rest of the taxidermenagerie, a fascinating exhibit on Adolph Topperwein, the greatest shot in history (he missed only 9 out of 72,500 wood blocks and was known for his gunshot art), an extensive doorknocker collection, a church made of 50,000 matches, and the mounted crania of those well-known River Walk drinking buddies, Manboon and Horned Conehead. Plus, you can drink a beer from the bar while you look at all this stuff.

Texas Chupacabra
Cuero and vicinity
www.cuerochupacabra.com

If you believe the hype, Texas has its own Chupacabra (a.k.a goatsucker), a vampiric legend best known for sucking goats dry in Puerto Rico. In South Texas, sightings of long-nosed, snaggle-toothed beasts that look like miniature mammalian *T-Rexes* are not uncommon.

Cuero resident and local businesswoman Phylis Canion has been tirelessly pursuing the alleged monster through the

South Texas brush for years. Canion came into possession of a dead specimen in 2007 and started selling Chupacabra T-shirts, hats, signs, and charms at her 7C Unlimited store (123 W. Main St., Cuero, 361-275-2015).

But to be truly informed on the matter, you really need to see the crazy footage (which CNN aired) a cop shot outside Cuero as he tailed an alleged Chupacabra. The video features a critter with burly haunches, short front legs, and a snout from here to kingdom come. Some say it's a coyote with a bad case of mange. I say it's an authentic Chupacabra. Prove me wrong.

El Muerto:
The Headless Horseman of South Texas
Uvalde and vicinity

El Muerto is a South Texas ghost story. As legend has it, a posse decapitated a particularly devious Mexican bandit in 1850 and strapped his body back into his saddle with his head in his lap as a warning to other would-be South Texas ne'er-do-wells. The bandit's black horse was said to scare folks for years with his ever-more-horrifying cargo, but locals eventually caught up with it and gave the bandit a proper burial. The bandit's ghost, however, is said to still ride the South Texas plains.

GRUB

Smokin' Joe's BBQ
Near Mission, twenty-six miles west of Brownsville

Barbecue on the border doesn't get any better. Smokin' Joe—a.k.a. José Martinez III—smokes his meat with mesquite alongside a *resaca* teeming with bass and catfish. Get yourself some ribs and sausage, a cold beer, and side dishes and a seat at one of the picnic tables under the big live oak tree, and wait for the sun to set on the horizon over the Rio Grande.

Birthplace of the Frito
San Antonio

Charles Elmer Doolin was just another confectioner before he bought a corn chip made from fried *masa* at a San Antonio gas station. It was 1932. The country, in the throes of the Great Depression, demanded cheap junk food. Doolin sensed an opportunity to make snack-food history and bought the business from the Mexican man who was frying and bagging the chips. Legend holds that his mother perfected the recipe in a San Antonio kitchen, and the Frito was born.

Some say Katherine Doolin, C. E.'s wife, invented Frito Pie, but there are plenty who claim that New Mexico, not Texas, is the birthplace of that Southwestern delicacy of chili and Fritos and cheese. Not many fatty-food historians dispute, however, that she was the sole inventor of Fritos Chocolate Crunchies: crushed Fritos immobilized in chocolate on a cookie sheet.

The Pig Stand: The Last, First Drive-In
1508 Broadway, San Antonio
210-222-2794

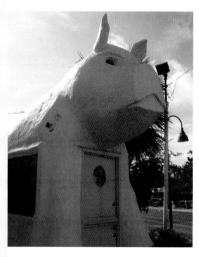

While the biomimetic porcines that once dotted Texas are now few and far between, you can still count on this San Antonio location. However, the pig-shaped architecture has been abandoned as other locations closed. The Broadway Pig Stand is a classic diner, but it doesn't look like a pig like some of the shuttered classics. This, the first Pig Stand—and thus the first drive-in—opened in 1921, a milestone year in the country's obesity epidemic. Other firsts: the first carhops and the first deep-fried onion rings.

SLEEPS

Chapeño: Larry and Babs's Place
Falcon Heights
956-848-5722

This is a great spot near binational Falcon Lake to get away from it all, complete with a little river frontage and a great little pool, amidst a fascinating, perpetually unfinished river compound. Chapeño is the brainchild of Larry "Loco Lorenzo" Barnett, who's been hanging out here and partying on the Rio Grande for a quarter of a century or so. Many of the overnight guests are birdwatchers, but watch out for Larry, who's been known to hang out in the river in his birthday suit. Highly recommended: tequila shots with Larry after the sun goes down. He's settled down a bit since hooking up with his significant other, Babs, a few years ago, but he's still at least a little bit loco.

MISC.

Los Ebanos Ferry
FM 886 and the Rio Grande, Los Ebanos
956-485-2855

In operation since the 1740s, this last hand-pulled ferry on the Rio Grande is a throwback—and threatened by the ever-more-militarized US–Mexico border. With a capacity of three cars and twelve people, this ferry is the only man-powered method left to legally cross the Rio Grande. After the political overreaction that shut down the paddle-powered crossings at Paso Lajitas, Boquillas, and Santa Elena in the Big Bend, this is the only way to get across the river under someone else's power.

Museum of the Republic of the Rio Grande
1005 Zaragoza St. on San Agustin Plaza, Laredo
956-727-3480

The popular phrase *Six Flags over Texas* discounts the little-known seventh flag that once flew over what is now Texas soil. This museum on San Agustin Plaza in downtown Laredo focuses on that flag, that of the Republic of the Rio Grande. Emboldened by the Republic of Texas, the locals seceded from Santa Anna's Mexico and became the Republic of the Rio Grande from January 17, 1840, to November 6, 1840. Laredo was the short-lived republic's capital city—in fact, the museum is in the historic (and modest) capitol building. The whole thing fell apart after forty weeks and three days, when a local military commander dropped his support of the republic in exchange for a top job in the Mexican army. But their flag proudly remains in the plaza alongside its six better-known and longer-lasting peers.

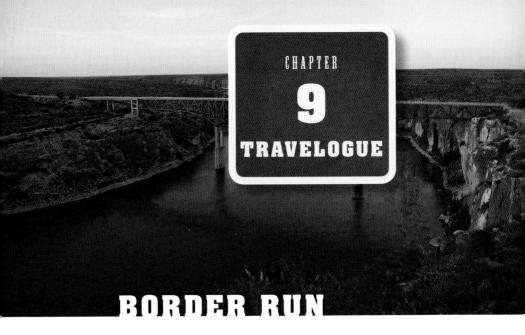

CHAPTER 9 TRAVELOGUE

BORDER RUN

6 DAYS, ABOUT 1,200 MILES, TWO COUNTRIES

The sun smoldering on the western horizon behind us, we speed toward the southernmost tip of Texas: Boca Chica. Spanish for "small mouth," Boca Chica is where the Rio Grande meets the Gulf of Mexico, about thirty miles west of Brownsville, Texas, and about thirty shallow feet north of Mexico.

Diana Joe drives her SUV along the beach toward land's end. My traveling cohort, Jay J. Johnson-Castro Sr., rides shotgun, while I sit in the backseat with John Neck, a wily third-generation Brownsville resident who served with the US Marines in Vietnam and crabbed the Rio Grande.

Passing house-sized dunes on our right and families playing and fishermen casting in the surf to our left, we keep going until the Rio Grande blocks our route. Across the shallow water, Mexican families and fishermen are playing and casting too.

We clamber out of the car for snapshots before the last sliver of sun melts from sight. A guy across the river whistles and yells for me to take his picture, so I do. He keeps on yelling and whistling.

Night takes hold, and we retreat back up the beach a mile or so for a few beers and some conversation. I join Diana wading in the water. "The ocean is a great spirit," she tells me. "It does a lot for us. *Del agua, al agua.* From the water, to the water."

Diana was born and raised in the area, born twelfth of sixteen kids to an Anglo father and a Yaqui Indian mother.

Boca Chica

She'd met Jay a month earlier, during his 205-mile walk from Laredo to Brownsville, his personal protest against legislation signed in October 2006 to build 700 miles of walls along the border. John had followed Jay in his pickup truck, helping with food, water, Band-Aids, and moral support. A wall would cut off sister cities up and down the Rio Grande Valley and beyond, Diana, John, and Jay all agree.

"The decision to build a wall down here was not democratic," Jay told me as we drove from Del Rio (his place of residence and the location of his B&B, the Villa Del Rio) to Brownsville. "It's dictatorial. It's tyrannical. It's immoral."

Jay had finished his walk a few weeks before our trip and then followed it up with a sixty-mile walk from Ciudad Acuña to Piedras Negras on the Mexican side. On this trip, his feet are still blistered and his throat still hoarse from talking and breathing dusty fumes, but his antipathy against the idea of a wall on the river still rages strong.

Jay's passion for the border makes him an ideal companion on this particular journey. On our way south, we'd made a few stops—the plaza in Laredo, the spectacular river view in Roma, and a late lunch of enchiladas and tostadas in a little café surrounded by lush Rio Grande Valley farmland—but mostly maintained my Saturn's velocity to make it to the Gulf of Mexico by sunset. Jay and I met John and Diana a few minutes ago, in a gas station parking lot a few miles up the road.

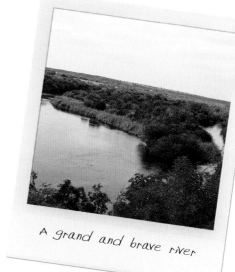

A grand and brave river

Down at Boca Chica, with the narrow, shallow channel that is the border, and where kids are playing and fishermen fishing on both sides, the idea of a wall feels beyond ridiculous.

"What people in faraway places of power don't understand is we don't want a wall," says John, after I retreat from my wade in the surf with Diana to solid ground. John's a third-generation Anglo American resident of the Brownsville area and a serious history buff. "We get along down here. Brownsville depends on Matamoros, and Matamoros depends on Brownsville."

"The image is that the only people on the border are smugglers and cops trying to catch them, with frequent and bloody shoot-outs," he adds. "That just isn't the case."

We talk on the beach until our stomachs growl and then drive back to the gas station where John and I left our cars. En route, we pass through a US Border Patrol checkpoint where an agent asks about our citizenship first and waves us through second.

We pay a visit to Diana's mother, Gloria Lucas, an octogenarian who oversaw the birth of more than 20,000 border babies as a midwife. She warmly thanks Jay for his protest walk. She wanted to walk with him for a day, but her family convinced her otherwise, as she had been ordered by her doctor to use a walker. (She tells us it gathers dust in a closet.)

"Poor people need to cross the river," she says. "Thank you for doing what you're doing. We don't want that wall."

John heads home, and Diana, Jay, and I convoy to the residence of Maria Elena Lucas, Diana's older sister. Her house is a bit ramshackle, but comfortable and chock full of interesting stuff (a longhorn skull, Yaqui artifacts, and an antique unopened bottle of sugar cane liquor with a distinctive leaf sunk in it, to name a few). In her sixties, Maria Elena mentions she is in the process of divorcing a husband who is thirty years her junior. She graciously makes dinner and the four of us talk into the night.

Diana Joe and Maria Elena

I soon realize there is far more to Maria Elena than what first meets the eye. I learn that she makes killer salsa, more than a little spicy. I also learn that she once worked as a migrant farmworker with seven kids (and no husband) in tow, and "was almost excommunicated from the Catholic Church" for speaking out for workers' rights. She fought back and helped organize other workers, predominately Mexican women. "It got to the point where we realized we were slaves," she says. The industry blacklisted her, but she fought on, becoming a representative of César Chávez. In the late 1980s, she was poisoned by pesticides when a barrel on a crop duster disintegrated while flying above her. "I died three times," she tells us. (If this sounds to you like the makings of one hell of a biography, you're right: *Forged under the Sun / Forjada bajo el sol: The Life of Maria Elena Lucas* was first published in 1993.)

After hearing Maria Elena's fascinating story, the conversation turns back to the concept of a border wall. The Berlin Wall didn't work, we all agree. Same goes for the Great Wall of China.

Diana makes the point that the Yaqui people are split by the US–Mexico border, a unique distinction. "I am personally offended," she says of the wall, "because I consider the river sacred."

Maria Elena is an unbelievably gracious host. She gives me her bed while Jay takes the couch and she and Diana sleep on an inflatable mattress. In the morning, she makes us an amazing breakfast of eggs, potatoes, sausage, more of her killer salsa, and piping-hot homemade tortillas. "I don't know how many thousands or millions of women make tortillas, and they all use the same ingredients, but they all come out differently," she laughs.

Diana tells us the tequila worm is actually "a sacred symbol of how man and nature worked together." The sisters then talk about tamale making and how an uncooked tamale (a pinto) means one of the women involved in its preparation is pregnant. The conversation veers to traditional ways of detecting an unborn child's sex and a mother's uncanny ability to do just that, and then back to the plight of the poor people on both sides of the Rio Grande. "If there's going to be any changes, it's going to be the women," concludes Maria Elena.

After breakfast, Diana loads her hand-carved Lakota peace pipe with flowers and herbs, telling us how it was custom-made for her by a tribal elder and she was never questioned about it when she crossed the border, bound north or south. The four of us smoke in silence, observing ancient traditions Diana strives to keep alive.

We bid the sisters good-bye and drive to meet back up with John Neck at the nearby Palo Alto Battlefield National Historic Site, where the first battle of the Mexican-American War took place on May 8, 1846. The displays depict what happened here that day as an act of military aggression by the United States, a violent landgrab that resulted in Mexico losing half of its acreage and the United States gaining not only Texas, but also the future states of California, Colorado, New Mexico, and Arizona.

I walk out onto the hot, humid battlefield, thick with thorny and prickly greenery. It strikes me that most of the West as we know it was Mexico 160 years ago, a mere blink of Father Time's eye. The meandering border of the Rio Grande—or Rio Bravo, as it's known in Mexico—is a relatively new concept, and an arbitrary one. Heading back to the visitor center, I'm very happy to spot an increasingly rare Texas horned lizard, better known as a horny toad.

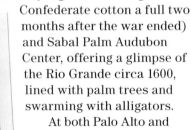

Prickly pears

From Palo Alto, John, Jay, and I hit a couple of spots near Boca Chica: Palmito Hill, site of the last battle of the Civil War (fought over a barge of Confederate cotton a full two months after the war ended) and Sabal Palm Audubon Center, offering a glimpse of the Rio Grande circa 1600, lined with palm trees and swarming with alligators.

At both Palo Alto and Sabal Palm, Jay receives VIP treatment from employees as "the guy who walked from Laredo to Brownsville." No one we meet, not even federal employees, voices one iota of support for the concept of a wall.

Sabal palms

Then it is time for us to cross the border. I drive my Saturn through the bustling metroplex of Brownsville-McAllen in the Rio Grande Valley, home to 6 million people on both sides, roughly the same as the San Francisco Bay Area. "When I was a kid, these were all separate towns," John observes. "Now it's like California. That's a sign of prosperity."

We cross the bridge between Brownsville and Matamoros and zip through the latter's snazzy plaza, more vibrant than downtown Brownsville or the outlying commercial strips, an indistinct collection of plastic and neon that at times defies place and culture.

As I drive, Jay dubs the Texas–Mexico border "the bastard child of Texas, and the bastard child of the United States." John defends undocumented immigrants working in the United States, noting that the economy of Mexico is comparable to that of the US during the Great Depression.

From the heart of Matamoros, we drive an hour east, trading urban civilization for rural farmland and rural farmland for the beach (a.k.a. Playa Bagdad). John buys a six-pack of Modelo at a colorful bazaar of bars and other businesses.

Then we drive on the beach the remaining few miles to the other side of Boca Chica, a literal stone's throw from where we watched the sun set the night before. It required over two hours to legally cross the river into Mexico and drive back to land's end at the Gulf. If we'd illegally waded the mouth of the Rio Grande into Mexico, it would have taken less than a minute to get to the same exact place.

We watch the herons and the fishermen and the brilliant sunset over the river, the Gulf of Mexico shimmering in the last light.

En route back to Brownsville, I learn a hard lesson about the enormous Mexican speed bumps known as *topés*, screeching to avoid hitting one at thirty-five miles an hour. "This is Mexico! Slow down!" John bellows. I struggle in vain to find that elusive balance of aggressiveness and guardedness that seems to be second nature to Mexican drivers.

After uneventfully passing through customs back into Texas, we zoom north to Las Milipas, where Jay had arranged for us to stay at the home of Fabio and Virginia, a couple he met during his walk. Fabio is a planner with the adjacent city of Pharr, and Virginia is a legal advocate for immigrants and workers.

Rio Grande sunset

Before we dig into a meal of chicken and mashed potatoes, their seven-year-old son, Noah, shows me his bug collection, which includes a grape-sized tarantula. Several people who had been involved with Jay's walk, including Diana Joe and two local journalists, meet us at the house, and the ensuing conversation runs the gamut from border politics to the native Mexican translation of *avocado* (testicle).

"Japanese and European multinationals like to invest in Mexico," says Fabio. "American multinationals want to ship all of their profits back to the US."

The conversation turns to the push for a border wall. Everyone agrees the idea to be a political ploy and the reality to be an ecological disaster.

Notes John: "Anti-immigrant sentiment is a cyclical thing."

"Most people," echoes Fabio, "don't bother to learn history."

One of the journalists estimates that 90 percent of local residents oppose a border wall. Jay's harsh terminology—*fascist, tyrannical,* and so forth—sounds more apt by the minute.

The party dwindles and ends. This night Jay gets the spare bed and I get a mattress on the floor. The long day makes for a good night's sleep.

Before we leave the next morning, Virginia and Fabio tell Jay about a *maquila* (border factory) across the river in Reynosa that was exposing its workers, predominately women and children who were paid $60 a week, to toxic conditions. Even more nefarious, a whistle-blower had been shot.

"We have a right," says Fabio, "to say what goes on in American factories around the world."

From Las Milipas, Jay and I continue on our trip up the river. We cross into Mexico at Nuevo Progresso, a bustling shopping mall of a town, as Jay puts it, twenty square blocks of pharmacies, dentists, street vendors, pottery stores, and just about everything else, surrounded by farmland. All of the customers, not surprisingly, are Americans, most of them retirees. I consider buying a Mexican wrestler playset, but resist and soon regret the nonpurchase. We cross back north into the US and get thoroughly searched by a drug-sniffing dog and a pair of customs agents. They come up empty-handed, but cost us twenty minutes or so.

After the delay, we drive through McAllen and return into Mexico at Los Ebanos. The crossing here is official, complete with border agents on both sides, but there is no bridge. Instead, there's a hand-pulled ferry with a capacity of three cars and maybe a dozen pedestrians. A team of Mexicans with thick arms and leather gloves power the motorless barge by tugging on a cable strung across the river. A popular crossing point for centuries, it is the only such ferry on the Rio Grande/Rio Bravo, but there are rumors that it could be replaced by a bridge—which would

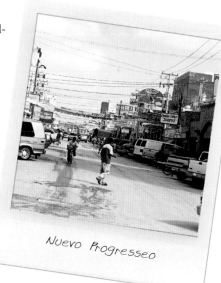

Nuevo Progresseo

mark the end of an era, but probably prove an economic
boon to communities on either side.

In Mexico, we continue on our northwestward journey,
weaving through road construction and heavy truck traffic.
We take a few minutes to drive the fascinating backstreets
of sleepy Ciudad Mier, one of the oldest communities in the
region, full of beautiful architecture, much of it crumbling.

Soon after we get back on the main highway, a trio of
federales, Mexican soldiers, flag us over to the side of the
road to search my trunk.

"No matter what," I say after they let us go, "a guy with a
machine gun is intimidating."

Jay corrects me. "A kid with a machine gun."

We cross back into the US on the bridge over Falcon
Lake, hightail it through Laredo to Del Rio, and arrive at
Jay's home and B&B, the Villa Del Rio, in time to watch the
second half of a comeback win by the San Antonio Spurs.

· · · · ·

We're weary, and my car needs an oil change, so we take our
time getting back on the road, leaving for El Paso around 11 AM
the next morning.

We had both spent time in El Paso before this trip, and
neither of us had been left with a very good impression.
Jay tells me he's generally averse to big cities and finds El
Paso in particular to be a car-clogged, culture-free sprawl.
I had visited several times, including once with my dad,
who'd been stationed in town at Fort Bliss in the 1960s. My
dad dubbed it the Detroit of the Southwest, and a negative
image lingered in my mind—although I have nothing
against Detroit.

The formidable distance between Del Rio and El Paso
makes for a day spent in motion more often than not. We
stop at the overlook of the Pecos River, with 300-foot cliffs
on either side as it snakes through the Texas Badlands and
joins the Rio Grande just to the south. We also stop to take
pictures of a drug blimp high in the sky west of Marfa.

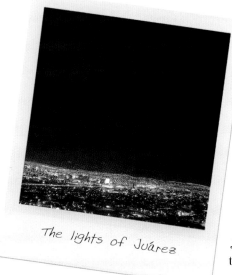

The lights of Juárez

We arrive in El Paso at the end of the workday and have dinner at my favorite Mexican joint on the planet, the L & J Cafe. A speakeasy during Prohibition, the L & J opened in 1927 and serves chicken enchiladas that are beyond words. After dinner, we drive around town, stopping at Rim Road Park, overlooking the twin cities. The lights of Juárez twinkle all the way to the southern horizon.

Next, Jay and I clink cold bottles of Lone Star at Rosa's Cantina (either the bar that inspired Marty Robbins's "El Paso" or the bar that was inspired by it). After draining our respective bottles, we call it a night.

· · · · ·

The next day is dedicated to the southern side of the border, Ciudad Juárez. With some 3 million residents, Juárez is three to four times the population of El Paso and, like much of Mexico, appears torn between the past and present. Jay and I get a ride across the free bridge (the downtown one charges a toll) with Pifas and Veronica from El Paso's tourism bureau. The line back into the US stretches on for about a mile.

"It's usually an hour and a half, an hour and forty-five minutes to cross," Pifas says, "and longer on holiday weekends. Easter weekend, don't even think about it."

But there is no line heading into Mexico. We get drinks and peruse menus at a new Frida Kahlo–themed restaurant mere minutes after crossing the bridge. Jay talks border politics, I order a stuffed poblano pepper with pomegranate sauce, and Pifas tells me he was born in El Paso and never had an itch to leave. "It still feels like a small town to me," he says. "Everyone knows everyone."

After lunch, we go to the Juárez Museum of Art, which has a nice display of contemporary work from Oaxaca, but smells funny and needs some serious maintenance (cracked tiles, empty water features, and other problems).

Onward toward the plaza, we pass a statue of a bullfighter fighting bulls in front of an empty lot. "It's really sad," says Veronica. "They demolished Monumental Bullring. I think Walmart is building there."

Legendary actor/kisser Tin-Tan

Some of Juárez rots, some of it gleams, and a good chunk looks to be perpetually under construction. Drug violence has started to mount. Veronica tells us that many factories have moved on to lower-cost labor markets, like Indonesia, but that the economy was still growing. A man juggles oranges at the red light and panhandles passing cars for change.

We go to the old market—geared exclusively toward gringo tourists—and wander around. Souvenirs beckon, velvet art, tacky ponchos, assorted statues, and brightly colored knickknacks. I try in vain to buy a plaster Elvis bust, finding the very same vendor where I'd purchased one four years earlier. (It shattered, then was reconstructed during band practice.) Alas, the vendor tells me they don't make them anymore. Like Nuevo Progresso, I leave the market empty-handed except for a tinge of regret.

Next we head over to the locals' market downtown, Mercado Reforma, and the inventory is much different, with booths hocking underwear and blow-dryers and pirated DVDs of Hollywood's latest.

As we stroll around, Veronica and Pifas ask if I'd seen the new statue in front of the El Paso International Airport, a larger-than-life Spaniard on a horse.

"The conquistador?" I ask.

They both recoil in horror. "Don't call it that!" Pifas said. "It's an equestrian!" They explain that the statue had been a source of controversy. It depicts Don Juan de Oñate, the leader of the late-sixteenth-century Spanish expedition that first crossed El Paso del Norte (the pass to the north) into modern-day Texas and New Mexico. Many locals objected on the grounds that de Oñate helped perpetrate genocide of native peoples. Thus, it was officially never to be referred to as a conquistador.

The Juárez plaza is vibrant and full of human activity. The historic Spanish mission on the plaza, established in 1668 and an active house of worship to this day, sits kitty-corner to a Wendy's. Domino's and Church's Fried Chicken are down the block.

Soon we cross back into the United States. From the middle of the bridge, El Paso's skyline, perfectly sunlit and set in front of the stark Franklin Mountains, is striking. A horde of Mexicans with shopping bags walk the other way.

Pifas and Veronica take us by Rocketbuster Boots, a maker of handmade custom boots that start around $750 a pair. After looking around at the velvet Elvii and the taxidermy and the World's Largest Cowboy Boots (4'6 3/4"), I ask Nevena Christi, one of the proprietors, about

Boots of art

her customers' requests. "They're never normal," she says, working on intricate bull and bear boots for a New York stockbroker. I look at a pair on her worktable, slick black-and-white numbers with all sorts of details. "Those are for Ethan Hawke."

Next we nose into a former boot factory, a huge brick building that had recently been reborn as OlO, the home of an arts nonprofit that worked with disadvantaged and disabled kids. The director, Stephen Ingle, gives us a tour. "You gotta give 'em options," he tells us. "A lot of kids we get here don't have a lot of money. It's something that El Paso needed, and I really love my job."

We race sunset to snap a photo of the Rio Grande, largely industrialized, more concrete than riverbank, snaking between the First World and the Third. Right across from hulking implements of heavy industry in Texas are the shanty-plastered hills of Juárez.

"That's Mexico," says Veronica. "You grow up in that poverty, looking over the river, you want to come over here."

After the sun is gone, Veronica and Pifas drop us off downtown. I briefly think my car is stolen and veer toward panic before Jay deftly points out that there are two levels in the garage. We cross into Juárez on foot for a margarita at the rumored birthplace of the drink, the Kentucky Club. As we walk past the quickly shuttering markets of downtown El Paso, I see cowboy boots in a bargain bin for $2.99, and think of Ethan Hawke. I quickly calculate that his boots cost at least 250 times as much.

The Kentucky Club is a timeless joint, decked out in ornate woodwork and neon, with a stuffed owl spread-winged

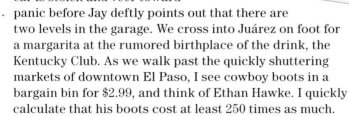

Border reflections

on a wall opposite the bar. Open since 1928—and serving such renowned drinkers as John Wayne, Steve McQueen, and Al Capone—legend holds that the margarita was invented here in the 1940s by longtime bartender Lorenzo Garcia.

I'd shaken Lorenzo's hand in 2002, briefly complimenting him on the drink. On this visit I learn he passed away in 2005. Jay and I toast Lorenzo with two of his inventions.

Jay talks with the bartender, Carlos, in Spanish, and asks him his opinion about the wall. "*No está bien*," Carlos replies. It's no good.

After our second margaritas, we decide to go back to our hotel. On the bridge back into El Paso, Jay stops and looks at the weak ribbon of water below, the Rio Grande, silently trickling amid the concrete and the barbed wire. A beggar on the Mexican side yells up and Jay drops him some change.

"Where is our river?" Jay quietly asks.

No longer open for business at 8 PM, downtown El Paso is the polar opposite of busy central Juárez. We wander into a festive karaoke mixer at the El Paso Museum of Art, a third-Thursday event. Young, upwardly mobile professionals drink and laugh and sing. An exhibition of black-and-white photographs examine the border's disparities, similarities, and symbioses. A placard informs me that Juárez residents spend $2 billion a month in El Paso.

We leave the border metropolis at 9 AM the next morning and head east against the last squalls of rush hour. From Van Horn, we backtrack to Marfa and then divert south to the border town of Presidio, and back

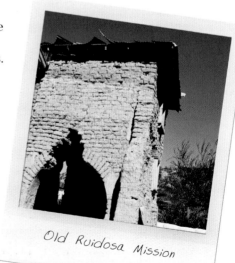

Old Ruidosa Mission

west on Farm Road 170. The paved road knifes back west toward El Paso, the Rio Grande to the south and the crags of the Chinati Mountains to the north. In an hour, we pass several beekeeping farms and a few ragged buildings, but only two or three cars. The pavement ends in Candelaria, forty-eight miles upriver from Presidio.

I turn left down a bumpy dirt road and follow it through a forest of salt cedar to the Rio Grande. The road dead-ends in a crude cul-de-sac fronted by a rickety footbridge. I park the car.

A sign warns that it is illegal to cross here.

We cross anyway.

Below the bridge, the river is surprisingly strong, perhaps the result of a recent thunderstorm. Five or six trucks, obviously those of commuters, are parked on the other side. Walking on Mexican soil feels good.

After illegally reentering the US, we pass a Border Patrol Jeep on the way back to Presidio, drive over the bridge into Ojinaga, and take a quick walk around the city center. It's splendid, a sleepy border town that isn't remotely Americanized. There's a sense of history and place that many American cities, dominated by fast food and car culture, have lost.

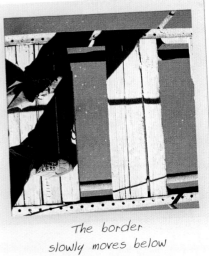

The border slowly moves below

We're back in Texas by 5 PM, driving east toward Lajitas, the luxury border golf resort where we had a room for the night. The rugged landscape, an undulating rocky desert cut in half by the rich blue-green of the river, glows.

"What a shame," Jay says.

"What?" I question.

"That side is a different country. I wish it was a whole."

We check into Lajitas at sunset, slurp bowls of tortilla soup at the bar, and watch the eye-opening documentary about the failed 2002 coup of Venezuelan President Hugo Chavez, *The Revolution Will Not Be Televised.*

In the morning we speak with Daniel, Lajitas's managing director. "The DEA is in here all the time," he says, labeling the notion of a wall ridiculous and like a prison.

Daniel tells us Lajitas employed a number of documented Mexicans who lived in a village a few miles south of the riverside resort. Before the Department of Homeland Security got involved, they crossed the river at Lajitas, taking five minutes to drive or row across. Now they can be prosecuted if they don't drive to Presidio, cross at the official bridge, and drive back to Lajitas—four or five hours in all.

"We used to have Christmas parties where the kids would come across," he adds. "We can't do that anymore. We have to send the presents over."

I drive Jay to Study Butte, where his innkeeper Sarah waits to give him a ride home to Del Rio. She takes our picture and we all hug good-bye. Great road trip, Jay and I agree.

I spend the remainder of my day hiking in Big Bend National Park, eating lunch in the shade of one of the knobby rock formations known as the Chimneys, before driving back to the river and the trailhead up Santa Elena Canyon.

Ojinaga Street

Jay enjoys a cerveza

The river lazily lulls through the masterwork of erosion it carved over an unfathomable period.

Excited, I half jog the trail to its end point, a sandy bank at water's edge. Looking upriver into the sunlit chasm, I breathe deep. This water, call it the Rio Bravo or the Rio Grande, is in no way a border. It is a river, and rivers are not boundaries. They outlive countries and governments. Rivers are—and have always been—lines of unity. Centers of commerce and culture. Gathering places.

Del agua, al agua.

I take off my boots and wade into the river. The cool water feels good on my feet.

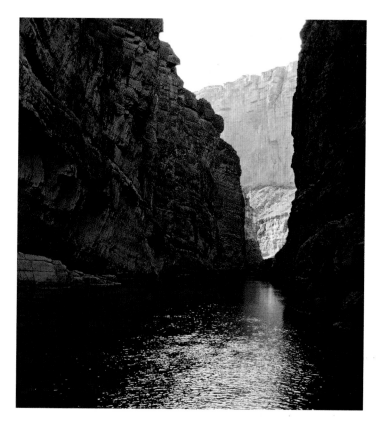

Where to go...

Boca Chica Beach
East of Brownsville,
at the east end of TX Hwy 4

**Palo Alto Battlefield
National Historic Site**
1623 Central Blvd.,
Brownsville
956-541-2785
www.nps.gov/paal

**Sabal Palm Audubon
Center**
8400 Southmost Rd.,
Brownsville
956-541-8034
www.sabalpalmaudubon.org

Playa Bagdad
Twenty-five miles east of
Matamoros, Tamaulipas

Villa Del Rio
123 Hudson Dr., Del Rio
800-995-1887
www.villadelrio.com

L & J Cafe
3622 E. Missouri Ave.,
El Paso
915-566-8418

Rim Road Park
Rim Rd., east of Mesa St.,
El Paso

Rosa's Cantina
3454 Doniphan Dr., El Paso
915-833-0402

Juárez Museum of Art
Lincoln Ave. and Ignacio Ave.,
Mejia, Ciudad Juárez,
Chihuahua

Rocketbuster Boots
115 S. Anthony St., El Paso
915-541-1300
www.rocketbusterboots.com

OlO Gallery
806 Montana Ave., El Paso
915-533-9575
www.creativekidsart.org

Kentucky Club
629 Avenida Juárez, Ciudad
Juárez, Chihuahua

El Paso Museum of Art
1 Arts Festival Plaza,
El Paso
915-532-1707
www.elpasoartmuseum.org

Lajitas Resort & Spa
HC 70, Lajitas
432-424-5000
www.lajitas.com

Big Bend National Park
East of Study Butte
432-477-2251
www.nps.gov/bibe

WEST TEXAS AND THE PANHANDLE

INTRODUCTION

This is the Texas of vast and wide nothingness, where gas stations are left to rot, where everything alive has fangs or needles or thorns, where sky and sun often perfectly intersect.

This is also the Texas of cotton fields, cattle, oil, and, of course, helium. Then there's the Panhandle's often tornado-strength wind—the blustery apple of T. Boone Pickens's eye, at least when oil prices were sky high—and rock-and-roll history in the form of Buddy Holly and Roy Orbison's home-towns of Lubbock and Wink.

And this is also the *Tejas* of green chile that can induce euphoria, and the setting of the biggest border towns in the world, El Paso and Ciudad Juárez, the urban manifestation of the West Texas border that is the polar opposite of that vast and empty Big Bend.

This is a place where worlds overlap.

One such confluence is the world of man and the world of wild. West of the Pecos River, the population density plummets. The Spanish conquistadors named this region *Despoblados*, the depopulated zone. There are 4 people per square mile in bustling Pecos County, 2 per square mile in Presidio County, and 1 or less in Brewster and Jeff Davis counties. For comparison's sake, there are about 1,200 people per square mile in New Jersey and 6,500 people per square mile in Singapore. Out here there's just that one shack, that one trailer, or that one lone house on a hill in the average passing landscape.

In fact, the least-populated zones of the depopulated zone is only slightly less populated than the 1.3 people per square mile of the Western Sahara and the 1.2 people in each of Alaska's many square miles, but, hey, it's busier than Greenland—their meager density is measured in square miles per person rather than the other way around.

STATS & FACTS

- The top of Guadalupe Peak in Guadalupe Mountains National Park is the highest point in Texas, at 8,749 feet above sea level.

- The Permian Basin pumped out 11.3 billion barrels of oil from 1928 to 1966 and another 3.6 billion barrels from 1967 to 1993. Permian Basin production peaked at 665 million barrels a year in the early 1970s and has since declined by more than 50 percent.

- The Odessa Meteor Crater, southwest of town, is the second largest meteor crater in the United States and sixth largest in the world.

- The Terlingua mine was once the third largest in the world, providing mercury for ammunition during World War I. Once ammo went electric, the mercury market collapsed and the town temporarily went ghost.

But why are there no people? For an answer to this question, I recommend a visit to the Despoblados in July, when the canyons of the Big Bend warm up to 150 degrees Fahrenheit.

With so few people, it's hard to divide Texas from Mexico out here—it's a rugged wilderness on both sides of the river—but farther west at El Paso del Norte, so named because it was the best pass to the north for Spanish explorers 400 years ago, the few become many and the differences between the two countries becomes stark.

Still the best pass for trucks and trains today, El Paso is another great overlap, only this zone, clad in concrete and blacktop, is bisected by a sharply defined line that is often topped with razor wire.

Of course, those same Spanish explorers who once crossed the *rio* here followed many of the same trails blazed by the natives that were favored by their conquistador predecessors—many of whom, namely Francisco Vásquez de Coronado, were in search of El Dorado, the fabled Lost City of Gold.

Vásquez de Coronado explored the plateau known as the Llano Estacado, which occupies much of what is now the Texas Panhandle.

He never found it. Me, I'm still looking.

Somehow I don't think Lubbock is the Lost City of Gold.

BIG THINGS AND OTHER ROAD ART

Chinati Foundation
1 Calvary Row, Marfa
432-729-4362
www.chinati.org

Fed up with the stifling Manhattan art scene, Donald Judd picked up stakes in 1972 and relocated to the absolute middle of nowhere: Marfa, Texas (pop. 2,500, give or take). He bought a few city blocks downtown and ended up taking the reins of the Chinati Foundation, a local arts organization, in 1985.

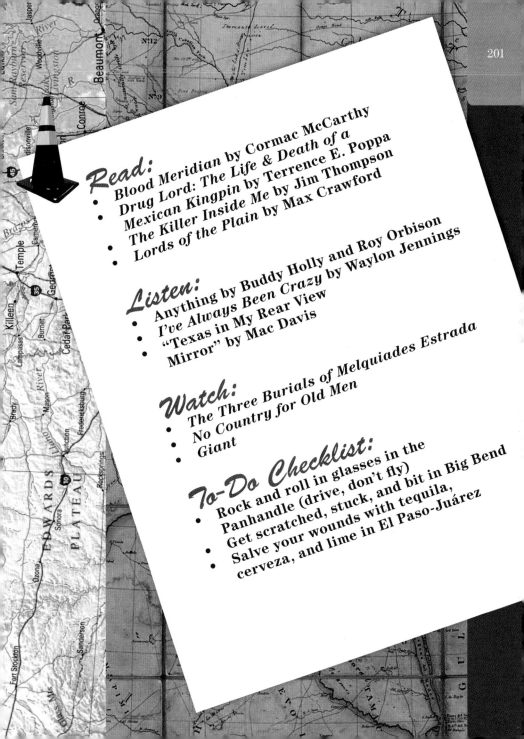

Read:
- Blood Meridian by Cormac McCarthy
- Drug Lord: The Life & Death of a Mexican Kingpin by Terrence E. Poppa
- The Killer Inside Me by Jim Thompson
- Lords of the Plain by Max Crawford

Listen:
- Anything by Buddy Holly and Roy Orbison
- I've Always Been Crazy by Waylon Jennings
- "Texas in My Rear View Mirror" by Mac Davis

Watch:
- The Three Burials of Melquiades Estrada
- No Country for Old Men
- Giant

To-Do Checklist:
- Rock and roll in glasses in the Panhandle (drive, don't fly)
- Get scratched, stuck, and bit in Big Bend
- Salve your wounds with tequila, cerveza, and lime in El Paso-Juárez

Judd installed some of his own work and also invited a few longtime buddies from the minimalist community to take part. The results are mind-boggling. The foundation's galleries are spread among the buildings at a former army post and a building in downtown Marfa, with Judd's massive concrete blocks out front, Dan Flavin's neon installations occupying no less than three former barracks structures, and John Chamberlain's crushed-car sculptures in the downtown gallery.

This has all culminated in Marfa being buzzed about in New York and LA as the next Taos, and cracked adobes that sold for $30,000 in 2000 were selling for five times that in 2005. But nothing will ever change the fact that Marfa is a remote Texas town that's only sixty-one miles north of the Mexican border. It's a bit slow for New Yorkers in the long run, unless they're cut from the same bullheaded cloth as Judd.

Cadillac Ranch
I-40, exit 60 or 62, west side of Amarillo

Oddly enough, these ten spray-painted Cadillacs on the side of the road are the American dynasty's equivalent of Egypt's

Great Pyramid at Cheops. At least that's the intent: Cadillac Ranch's automotive ingredients are buried up to their midsections at fifty-two degrees, the very same angle as the slope of its inspiration-sake pyramids across the planet.

A San Francisco art collective known as the Ant Farm initially installed Cadillac Ranch in 1974, under the financial and creative auspices of helium heir Stanley Marsh 3. (Yes, 3 not III. Stanley favors the Arabic numeral over the Roman standard.) It has since ascended into the holy pantheon of roadside Americana and even inspired a VW Bug copycat in the Bug Ranch in Conway, twenty miles east of Amarillo.

The Legs of Ozymandias
Just off I-27 at Sundown Ln., Amarillo
(Also brought to you by Stanley Marsh 3)

On the southern fringes of Amarillo sits a pair of disembodied legs, fronted by a plaque explaining their discovery by Percy Bysshe Shelley and his wife, Mary Wollstonecraft Shelley, here on the "Great Plains of New Spain." After the encounter, Bysshe Shelley wrote his famous poem "Ozymandias." "I met a traveler from an antique land," begins the poem, "who said two vast and trunkless legs of stone stand in the desert. Near them, on the sand, half sunk, a shattered visage lies." The plaque recites the poem in its entirety before explaining the statue was destroyed by students from Lubbock. A restoration is allegedly forthcoming.

"And on the pedestal these words appear: 'My name is Ozymandias, king of kings,: Look on my works, ye mighty and despair!' Nothing beside remains."

Floating Mesa
**Old Tascosa Rd. and TX Hwy. 1061,
about eight miles northwest of Amarillo**

Is that mesa levitating in the sky? Is it the work of telekinetic Venusians? Or is it a ring of sky blue plywood panels that makes the mesa apparently float on air? Only Stanley Marsh 3 knows for sure. (Hint: The prolific visionary oddball's most obscure art project only works when the sky is blue.)

Amarillo Signs
All over Amarillo, particularly near the Route 66 historic district in the Old San Jacinto neighborhood in northwest Amarillo

Another of Stanley Marsh 3's public-art projects involves a few hundred civic-looking signs with odd slogans. He made them freely available to people living in the community to proudly plant in front of their homes. Now the local yard art includes signs with all sorts of madcap slogans like, "Mime Assassin" and "Strong Drink Here" and two "No Two Signs Are Exactly Alike." I've also seen, "I Nurse the Barren Memory of Unkissed Kisses and Songs Never Sung" and "God Bless John Wayne."

Groom Cross
**Just off I-40, Groom
www.crossministries.net**

Like most Americans, I like my religious symbols big. The bigger, the better. I mean ridiculously big. Beyond huge. Fucking humongous.

In this vein, I present the Groom Cross, a crucifix 190 feet tall and weighing in at an impressive 2.5 million pounds. When it first rose on the Panhandle plains in 1995, it indeed was the biggest cross in the Western Hemisphere. Sadly, that title has since been swiped by a 198-foot cross in Effingham, Illinois, whose builders were inspired by the cross in Groom. What does the Bible say about one-upping thy neighbor?

Leaning Tower of Texas
Just off I-40, Groom

Faded paint displays Britten, USA, on this intentionally askew water tower that has seen many better days. This relic of 1950s Americana is the creation of Tower Fuel Stop proprietor Ralph Britten, who shortened the legs on one side of the tower for the eye-catching lean. The Route 66 landmark once meant you were fast approaching the middle of nowhere. Today, it provides a somewhat sad metaphor for the Panhandle in comparison with Pisa, or else just a good reason to pull off the interstate and take a picture.

World's Largest Jackrabbit
820 N. Sam Houston Ave., Odessa

In 1932, the same folks who brought you the Odessa Rodeo decided it would be a good idea to include a new event: the World's First Championship Jackrabbit Roping. This, of course, was a public relations disaster and an animal lover from Midland went as far as setting the participating jack-rabbits free. According to the plaque in front of the cockeyed jackrabbit in Odessa, which is said to be the largest in the world, the practice of roping jackrabbits came to an end in 1978 by a court order.

Paisano Pete: The World's Largest Roadrunner
US 290 at Main St., Fort Stockton

If you ever find yourself in Fort Stockton, I rec-ommend a visit with this big bird. And Pete, the world's largest roadrunner, is indeed plenty big, measuring twenty-two feet long and eleven feet in height. The 800-pound bird surely scares the wily coyotes much more than they scare him.

Paintbrush Alley
Between Concho and Twohig Aves., San Angelo

At this public mural gallery in downtown San Angelo, brick walls become canvases for a diverse array of murals, every-thing from workers on imaginary beams to cats on nonexis-tent windowsills.

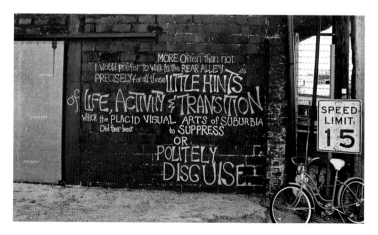

Fantasy Land Park
Alley Oop Ln., Iraan
432-639-2232

Alley Oop, the time-traveling caveman who's been the subject of the longest-running comic strip in the history of the world, has roots in West Texas's Permian Basin. V. T. Hamlin came up with the character while working at *The Des Moines Register* in 1932, drawing on his experience working in the oil fields around Iraan—no, not Iran, but in fact the names of the town's founding couple, Ira and Ann, smushed into one three-syllable word. In the 1960s, Iraan's town fathers wanted to honor Alley Oop's local origins and came up with the idea for Fantasy Land, a park with all sorts of rides and statues inspired by the comic. A statue of tame dinosaur Dinny was dedicated in 1965, and Alley Oop's oversized mug, sporting a top hat and smoking a cigar, followed a few years later. Hamlin came to Dinny's dedication, a docent told me. "He was quite a drinker," she added. "He had a big time." They never got around to any other statues, not Oola nor the Grand Wizer or Dr. Elbert Wonmug or King Guzzle or Queen Umpateedle, but the park's resident museum inside has a scrapbook full of old comic strips and a mannequin in a bizarre old hair-perm machine that looks like something out of *Barbarella*.

Stonehenge Replica
On the campus of University of
Texas of the Permian Basin, Odessa
432-552-2020

Texas has Stonehenge II, but it also has two Stonehenges. Not to be outdone by Hill Country's aforementioned Stonehenge II, the powers that be at the University of Texas of the Permian Basin funded their very own on-campus

Stonehenge replica in 2004. Unlike the pristine Hill Country version, this replica reflects the current state of the original Stonehenge on the Salisbury Plain, with formerly perched blocks lying askew on the ground. While the sense of awe and mystery is dimmed by the Home Depot in the backdrop, there are too few Stonehenge replicas to not visit every one you pass on your journey from there to here.

Plaza de los Lagartos
San Jacinto Plaza, Oregon St. and Mills Ave., El Paso

There used to be a fountain with real live alligators at this very spot in the middle of downtown El Paso. After their introduction in 1883—and subsequent breeding, kidnapping, and surfacing in a professor's office across town at UTEP, stoning, and enjoying breaks from the winter cold wrapped in coffee sacks in downtown saloons—the gators were deemed a threat to public safety and relocated to the El Paso Zoo. The plaza's Lagartos era is memorialized in the form of the late Luis Jimenez's vibrant sculptures of three of the reptiles.

R.I.P.

Buddy Holly, 1936–1959
Lubbock Cemetery
2011 E. 31st St., Lubbock

In the early days of rock and roll, Buddy Holly proved that geeks could rock as hard as anybody else. While the music industry has long focused on looks over sound, Holly had his trademark horn-rimmed glassed and the looks of an accountant. But he could play the hell out of his guitar and write killer songs—two skills Elvis notoriously lacked.

By the time the plane he chartered went down in a snowy Iowa cornfield, Holly was a certifiable rock icon—yet he was only twenty-two years old. The only item of Holly's recovered from the crash site were his trademark spectacles, now on display at the Buddy Holly Center in Lubbock. Besides his marker in Lubbock Cemetery, another place to pay tribute is the bigger-than-life statue perched across town on Avenue Q between 7th and 8th Streets.

John Wesley Hardin, 1853–1895
Concordia Cemetery
3700 Yandell Dr., El Paso

One of the most prolific killers of the Wild West, John Wesley Hardin claimed to have taken the lives of forty-four men. He also was a pathological liar, so that figure is unconfirmed. Small and ill-tempered, Hardin first killed when he was fifteen, shooting one of his uncle's former slaves. Then he went on the run, but instead of laying low got in numerous gunfights and killed three more men in no time. He practiced drawing his guns every day and had special holsters sewn into his vest. He killed many more before his arrest in 1877. Then he served seventeen years in prison, finished his law degree while incarcerated, and began practicing law in El Paso upon his release in 1894. Despite going legit, he earned a reputation for getting loaded and waving a gun, demanding his money back when he lost at cards. Soon thereafter, he was shot in the back of the head while playing dice at the Acme Saloon in El Paso. His grave is said to be El Paso's top tourist attraction.

Judge Roy Bean, circa 1825–1903
Whitehead Memorial Museum
1308 S. Main St., Del Rio
830-774-7568
www.whiteheadmuseum.org

Born Phantly Roy Bean, the self-described Law West of the Pecos poured drinks and dispensed justice at his saloon on the Rio Grande in West Texas. After a tumultuous marriage, a near-hanging, and several duels, Bean moved from San Antonio to a tent city near the confluence of the Pecos River and the Rio Grande named Vinegaroon, a nod to an ugly desert insect, and opened a bar. Because the nearest court was some 200 miles away in Fort Stockton, Bean got himself appointed justice of the peace in Pecos County and promptly used his newfound authority to riddle a competing saloon with bullets. Trying cases, he chose jurors from his bar stools and made often nonsensical decisions. He later moved west with the railroad construction and squatted on a little piece of land that came to be named Langtry, after East Coast actress Lily Langtry, whom he never met but had a major thing for. From his new saloon, Bean continued acting as JP, never imprisoning wrongdoers (Langtry had no jail), instead issuing fines (and two hangings) as punishment. He kept the money for himself.

VICE

La Kiva
FM 170, Terlingua
431-371-2250
www.lakiva.net

Established on Terlingua Creek by Gilbert Felts in 1981, this is one of the greatest bars in Texas. Where else can you get your drink on in a fake cave, sitting on a tree-stump bar stool? Where else can you eat barbecued meats while admiring a fossilized *Penisaurus erectus* specimen? Where else can you pee in a huge cast-iron pot? Only at La Kiva, that's where.

Starlight Theatre
Terlingua Ghostown
432-371-2326
www.starlighttheatre.com

The Starlight Theatre was a movie palace before it was shuttered along with the rest of Terlingua in the 1930s. Then the

STAR MAPS

- The Globe Theatre in Odessa is said to be the most accurate replica of William Shakespeare's home stage in the United States.

- Rosa's Cantina in El Paso (3454 Doniphan Dr., 915-833-0402) was either the inspiration for the Marty Robbins classic "El Paso" or else it was named for the focal watering hole of the song—nobody seems to remember which.

- In 1963, legendary rock-and-roll DJ Wolfman Jack first took to the airwaves across the river from Del Rio in 1963, on the world's most powerful radio station, XERF.

- Roy Orbison was born in Vernon, but grew up northwest of Odessa in Wink—thus the name of his first band, the Wink Westerners. Today, the Roy Orbison Museum (213 E. Hendricks Blvd., Wink, 915-527-3441) keeps Roy's legend alive—and you can slip on his trademark (and very powerful) prescription sunglasses for a photo op.

town slowly came back to life, and the Starlight was reborn as an extraordinary eatery/venue/bar in the 1990s, complete with dogs sniffing around and a shady front porch. The kitchen is known for its burgers, tacos, and cobbler, and the bar is renowned for its prickly pear margaritas. I heartily recommend all of the above.

Chilton

Once upon a time, one Dr. Chilton was at the Lubbock Country Club and wanted a cocktail that offered the proper refreshment from the harsh Panhandle summer. He instructed his bartender to mix the juice of two lemons with a vodka-and-club-soda cocktail, and serve it over ice in a glass with a salted rim. Today, Chilton's legacy lives on in the cocktail that bears his name and is widely available in Lubbock's bar scene. Most places skimp and only squeeze one lemon, but the Conference Cafe (3216 4th St., 806-747-7766) does the good doctor proud and throttles two.

Nightlife South of the Rio Grande

Across from Del Rio in Ciudad Acuña, the Corona Club (Hidalgo #200, www.coronaclubacuna.com) is owned by the Corona family of Corona cerveza fame and was featured prominently in the movie *Desperado* as the joint where Cheech Marin was the ornery bartender. In reality, the place is not nearly as grim as it was in the movie—especially the bathroom—and offers oodles of character (taxidermy and cool photos line the walls) and a massive courtyard out back. Across the river from El Paso in Ciudad Juárez, the Kentucky

Club (#629 Avenida Juárez) might just be the best place on the planet to hide out and swill margaritas. If you believe the legend, the margarita was invented here in 1946, by the late Lorenzo Garcia.

HUH?

Marfa Mystery Lights
Viewing platform on US 90, nine miles east of Marfa

Is it gas? Is it aliens? Ghosts? An optical illusion?

It's probably just gas. Between Marfa and Alpine on US Highway 90, you'll see a rest area with an unusual window cut into a solitary outdoor wall. At dark, you'll see why this particular rest area is so deluxe. On the horizon, bulbs of light appear on a nightly basis, then typically do a little dance, brighten a bit, and fade to black. Scientists have yet to come up with an explanation that placates everyone, thus the luminous globs' name: the Marfa Mystery Lights.

On some nights, the roadside viewing platform looks like a scene out of *Close Encounters*, loaded with gawkers of all kinds. Other nights, it's empty, with only the lights to keep the solitary onlooker company.

Robert Wood Johnson Museum of Frontier Medicine
**630 S. Oakes St.,
at the Fort Concho
National Historic Landmark,
San Angelo
325-481-2646
www.fortconcho.com**

If you ever wanted to know what they did to fix people up out here before they really knew how to fix people up, this is the place. The centerpiece is a pioneer ER, complete with mosquito nets and bedpans. Another display features some of the snake-oil remedies of the day, including a box of Dr. Bandit's Crotch Powder ("will prove serviceable for all kinds of ailments," the box explains). Also on hand: a Victorian prototype electro-stimulation gadget. Ever seen those freaky infomercials about gadgets that artificially induce facial spasms for muscle tone? This is its great-grandmother.

Replica of World's Largest Windmill
US 84 and XIT Ave., Littlefield

Measuring 132 feet in height with twelve-foot blades, the world's tallest windmill stood sentry on the sprawling XIT Ranch from 1887 until Thanksgiving Day in 1926, when a storm took out the wooden monolith. The town took it upon itself to commemorate its former claim to fame with a 114-foot version. Moral of the story: wooden windmills really should not be 132 feet tall.

GRUB

Big Texan Steak Ranch
7701 I-40 E., Amarillo
806-372-6000
www.bigtexan.com

Naturally, steaks in Texas have got to be bigger than steaks in any other state. And nobody goes bigger than Amarillo's Big Texan, the combination restaurant/entertainment emporium/ motel/gift shop/shooting gallery that has been the standard-bearer for Panhandle kitsch since it opened in 1960. As the billboards scream for miles in every direction, Eat a 72-ounce steak dinner and get it for free*!, with the asterisk being the price tag if you don't finish it in an hour—$72.

I have no interest in ever attempting to eat one myself. First off, it is four and a half pounds of red meat. Let me repeat that: four and a half pounds of red meat. Plus, you have to finish a salad and a baked potato. More than 60,000 people have attempted this feat in Big Texan's history, and about one in eight manages to pack away the whole slab of meat. The superlatives: a competitive eater apparently polished one off in less than ten minutes, and 368-pound wrestler Klondike Bill once ate two steaks in the allotted sixty minutes.

On separate occasions, I watched an unhappy Australian fail miserably, and I also watched a guy from the Ozarks, with twenty-three minutes to spare, became the 8,479th person to accomplish the task.

"How do you feel?" I asked.

"Terrible," he replied, hunched over.

"I won't burp you," said the manager.

El Paso: Mexican Food Bender

If you, like me, are a stone-cold fiend for spicy green chile and salsa, El Paso is one of the best places to get a truly satisfactory fix. For breakfast, hit the H & H Car Wash and Coffee Shop (701 E. Yandell Dr., 915-533-1144) for breakfast tacos or carne picada. In need of something tasty for lunch or dinner, you can't miss at the L & J Cafe (3622 E. Missouri Ave., 915-566-8418), a onetime speakeasy, now with a fourth generation of the Duran family plating up transcendent chicken enchiladas and huevos. Dusk or later, I like The Tap (408 E. San Antonio Ave., 915-532-1848) for a cold beer and the chile rellenos.

Birthplace of the Nachos: Piedras Negras or Ciudad Acuña?

Ignacio "Nacho" Anaya invented the nacho. The question is, where? Was it Crosby's, in Ciudad Acuña (#195 Hidalgo) or was it the Victory Club, now Moderno Restaurant, in Piedras Negras (#407 Allende)? Whatever the case, as the story goes, some drunken patrons wanted something simple to eat and

Anaya obliged by slicing up a leftover fried tortilla, adding cheese and jalapeños, calling it Nachos Especiales. It was later shortened to *nachos*, and you will find a plaque affirming Anaya's culinary landmark as taking place at Moderno in 1940. The people down the road at Crosby's beg to differ. You'll find phenomenal nachos, however, at both places, and good margs to toast Anaya, to boot.

SLEEPS

Thunderbird Marfa
601 W. San Antonio St., Marfa
877-729-1984
www.thunderbirdmarfa.com

A roadside motel reborn as a slick boutique lodging, the Thunderbird is a study in minimalist design, with its clean and modern rooms housing sleek furnishings and decor. Perks like record players, typewriters, and cruiser bikes are available through the front desk.

Gardner Hotel
311 E. Franklin Ave., El Paso
915-532-3661
www.gardnerhotel.com

I really like this inexpensive historic hotel turned budget lodging in downtown El Paso. So did John Dillinger, who stayed here while on the lam in the 1930s. The oldest operating hotel in the city, the Gardner has hostel bunks and comfy-but-dinky private rooms.

MISC.

Balmorhea Pool at Balmorhea State Park
Just south of Balmorhea
432-375-2370
www.tpwd.state.tx.us

A Civilian Conservation Corps project that opened to swimmers in 1941, this true desert oasis is fed by San Solomon Springs, which delivers a million gallons of water an hour—

enough water to fill the 1.75-acre pool in under four hours. Besides having one of the coolest names ever, the 75-degree-Fahrenheit pool is popular with not only swimmers, but also scuba divers: it melds classical and man-made in the water's edge with a thoroughly wild center teeming with fish above its rocky bottom.

Big Bend National Park
100 miles south of Alpine
432-477-2251
www.nps.gov/bibe

This is it: desert wilderness extraordinaire. Centered on the rumpled majesty of the Chisos Mountains, the park is known for its brutal beauty and sheer canyons on its southern border, the Rio Grande. And with a furred and feathered population that includes black bears, wild desert pigs known as javelinas, scorpions, and tarantulas, this is clearly a place where you can get away from other people.

Guadalupe Mountains National Park
About sixty miles north of Van Horn
915-828-3251
www.nps.gov/gumo

Big Bend's northern cousin is a former undersea reef that has come full circle over the last 250 million years or so, undergoing a metamorphosis into the canyon-laden desert mountains you see today. It is one of the least-visited national parks in the system, so come prepared, because this is truly the middle of nowhere. And bring your hiking boots.

WEST TEXAS RAMBLE

FIVE DAYS, 250 MILES, PLENTY OF SOLITUDE

Drifting in the sun-jeweled waters, it's a fall afternoon. The water is warmer than the high-desert air.

A school of tiny fish surrounds me. They are totally unafraid. Even when I swim and paddle, they immediately return to my side, attracted by some invisible lure, pheromones or drowning microorganisms or shedding flakes of skin.

I stop and float, dead in the water. Hundreds of three-inch fish swarm my right hand. Then they start nibbling on my fingertips. One briefly chomps on my nipple. At least it doesn't hurt.

Ouch! One of the little fuckers just bit a sensitive spot on my back.

I swim into the shallows of the pool and walk on the algae-covered bottom once my feet can touch. My gaze goes down. My feet are shockingly white. I need to tan them on this ramble into the West Texas borderlands.

Besides feeling the need for a good foot tan, I also feel a vague need to purify myself. I'm in a rut, my car is a complete mess, and I've been on the road for too long. The pool is a good start.

Floating on my back again, I mentally drift back to the morning. I'd spent the night in Midland and left around noon, heading south. I got a good look at the industrial landscape of Texas oil country, occasional vistas of a rugged land dominated by machinery. Farther south, the gears and pumps fade and the landscape takes over.

Now I'm swimming in the Y-shaped pool at Balmorhea State Park in West Texas, fed by San Solomon Spring, a natural desert oasis and a 1930s-era public works project rolled into one. The man-made pool has a classical design, a rocky floor, and fish and other aquatic inhabitants. I climb out and dry myself in the warm sun and cool breeze.

Leaving, I pass an interpretive display covering some frequently asked questions about the pool. "How much water comes out of the spring? An average of a million gallons per hour (less during droughts). The 3.5-million-gallon pool takes about four hours to fill."

The million-gallon reference mentally rewinds me two hours to the Million Barrel Museum in Monahans, about seventy-five miles northeast of Balmorhea. Here, in the 1930s, Shell Oil warehoused, yes, a million barrels in a huge, leaky concrete tank topped with a huge wooden shell. They emptied it once the government started taxing belowground reserves. Now you can drive your car down into the drained reservoir or spray-paint your name and graduation year on its walls. I opted for only the former.

Back in the present, I'm driving south from Balmorhea to Fort Davis. Sunlight glimmers on the gently rippling

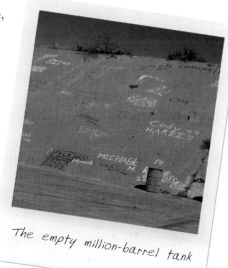

The empty million-barrel tank

green and gold leaves on the trees in the foreground, at the same time emphasizing every fold and crag in the undulating and rocky backdrop.

The road is nearly devoid of traffic. Authorized Personnel Only reads a sign on the fence surrounding a junkyard just north of town. Beyond the quaint storefronts and bed-and-breakfasts in Fort Davis, the sun soaks into the western horizon as the eastern sky turns purple and blue. The West Texas dusk is a work of art.

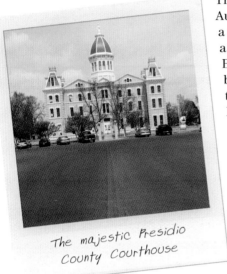

The majestic Presidio County Courthouse

Soon the unmistakable Marfa skyline—consisting in its entirety of a water tower and the Presidio County Courthouse—comes into view. I drive to the eastern fringe of town to look at the sky's darkening hue before it goes black, then meander for fifteen minutes trying to locate my friend Gary Oliver's house.

A Marfa resident for more than twenty years, Gary is the cartoonist for *The Big Bend Sentinel*. His specialty is the devastating political cartoons on border issues, and many focus on environmental controversies. He's also a great musician, with his roots in the 1970s Austin scene, and an extremely well-traveled guy who tells me he'd sleep in the bushes before he would pay more than a buck for a room. Here at his adobe house, which he bought for $5,000 in the early 1980s, just outside of Marfa city limits, Gary's got a major home improvement project underway: a half-finished addition with a floor of bricks and earth.

I greet him with a six-pack of Shiner Bock and a 99¢ bag of Fritos, then tell him I'm looking to get away somewhere around Big Bend, really get away. Even the national park will be too crowded. "I need a good vision quest."

West Texas sunset

Keying me into a piece of property he owns north of the park, Gary says that West Texas is some of the best unspoiled wilderness in the country, but not a major tourist destination because the two national parks—Guadalupe Mountains and Big Bend—are too far apart. Right-wingers around Fort Davis killed a survey that would have looked at possibilities for another park of some kind in the Davis Mountains. A park in that vicinity could create a critical mass of parks that attracts visitors from all over the world, not unlike Utah, says Gary, lamenting, "The property-rights assholes wouldn't even let them look into it."

The sheer size of West Texas comes up. Gary says that 50 percent of Texas State Parks's land is one parcel: Big Bend Ranch State Park, just west of the national park. "You're in a county that is bigger than Delaware and Rhode Island together. Right next door, Brewster County is bigger than Connecticut."

And there are few people, just 50,000 in five counties immediately west of the Pecos River. This is the land seventeenth-century Spanish explorers nicknamed *Despoblados*—the depopulated zone.

This is obviously a great lure for people trying to distance themselves from humanity, whether it is for a night or a lifetime. But it's also a great lure for polluters, Gary notes. He has personally dedicated a good deal of his time in recent years fighting Texas nuclear-waste dumps tooth and nail, and he helped kill a proposal for one in nearby Sierra Blanca in 1998.

"People have given up their lives, their relationships, their jobs to fight this," he says, explaining the bureaucratic trickery the state employed to push for the dump. "Everything bad about democracy we do in excess in Texas."

George W. Bush was then Texas's governor, and the Sierra Blanca proposal became a political albatross he had to shed in order to win the Hispanic vote in his impending bid for the presidency. "He couldn't show his face in the western part of the state without a demonstration," says Gary. "Once, we had a kid in a gas mask and a sign painted, 'I want to live.' Even at a press conference about West Texas tourism, a reporter asked him, 'Do you think nuclear waste is good for tourism?'"

Six empty bottles of Shiner later, I crash in a guest house in Gary's ramshackle backyard. The overnight low temperature is below freezing and the heater-free guest house gets pretty close. My sleeping bag keeps most of my body warm most of the night.

Gary's happy dogs, black-and-white-Lab mixes, greet me when I come in the back door for coffee the next morning. I get a cup and sit down with Gary, who tells me about the sludge waste from the New York sewer system they used to ship to West Texas, plays me a few songs (Bill Staines's "All God's Critters" and Richard Thompson's "Wall of Death," with a few special modifications relating it to the increasingly walled US–Mexico border), and gives me directions to his property near Big Bend. In turn, I help him hang some tar paper on his new addition, then take a shower and hit the road.

The drive to Alpine goes by quickly. It's a warm, quiet afternoon in the colorful college town, home of Sul Ross University. On campus is the Museum of the Big Bend. I stop for a look. A plane-sized pterosaur with a fifty-foot wingspan hangs in the rafters, with a cast of the bone that inspired the scale model under glass below.

One display covers Álvar Núñez Cabeza de Vaca, the first European to visit the Big Bend region. His scouting party dwindled from 300 conquistadors landing in Florida in 1528 to three running for their lives in Tejas. After seven years on the lam, including one stint imprisoned by unfriendly locals and another as a wandering healer, Cabeza de Vaca (yes, his surname means "cow's head") made his way to the Big Bend region and found the Jumanos to be the "best-looking" people he'd yet encountered—perhaps he was just getting a little lonely. A year later, he finally reconnected with some Spanish cohorts at a Pacific outpost and headed back home.

Another exhibit focuses on the first US attempts to map Big Bend in the 1850s. It was brutal. "The party lost mules, boats, and supplies, and ultimately suspended the expedition," the display explains. Next came the army and the Indian wars, heavy bloodshed in a sparsely populated land.

I follow the time line around the faux rock landscape of the museum, from Big Bend's 10,000-acre incarnation as a state park in 1933 before becoming a 150,000-acre national park two years later. The additional 140,000 acres were repossessed from landowners who hadn't paid their taxes.

A voice-over on a video explains, "It's been described as both God's country and the Devil's playground."

Then I check out a display on Tall Rockshelter. In a remote canyon in the Davis Mountains, forty-foot-tall paintings of abstract red figures dominate a wall, their meaning unknown. Next to a re-creation of the rock art, there is a quote from Robert Mallouf, director of the Center for Big Bend Studies at Sul Ross: "There are archaeological sites out there that defy the scientist's dry and disciplined logic—sites that cannot help but instill a sense of awe and mystery in the human consciousness. Tall Rockshelter is such a site."

La Frontera

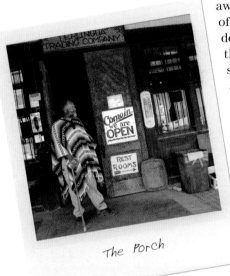

The Porch

I veer south, the vegetation fades away, and the rock angrily claws out of the scorched earth. A tarantula deliberately crosses the road. At the collection of motels and gas stations at an intersection that is for all practical purposes downtown Study Butte, I bear right and drive five more miles to Terlingua. The mercury-mining town turned ghost town when the mines closed, but then was reclaimed by hippies and artists and eccentrics in the 1970s. Now it's a living town—well, except for summertime, when temperatures hover around 120 degrees and the population dips to double digits—full of ruins and rebuilt ruins.

After checking in to a room at La Posada Milagro, above town with a commanding view of the Chisos Mountains, I have dinner at La Kiva, a local fake cave/bar/ barbecue joint, and end up at the smoky Boathouse, with chipped concrete floors, a number of dogs, and walls clad in dilapidated billboards for local rafting companies.

Sitting on the nearly broken bar stool, I talk with a British guy named Ralph who spends several months a year in Terlingua. He tells me he is not at all looking forward to going back to England in a few days.

Terlingua is not for everybody, he says. "Some people move here and don't make it two years. Some people couldn't make it anywhere else.

"But people really, truly look out for each other. There's this guy here, Uh Klem. That's not his real name, that's just what he calls himself. Uh. He's going blind but people help him get along."

Ralph pauses, then adds, "He drinks a case of beer a day."

The next morning, I wander over to my friend Cynta's for coffee. She lives in a beautiful house overlooking Terlingua, with a view stretching for miles, mountains and crags in all directions.

Cynta tells me she is working to set up Terlingua Arms, a local retirement community, for Klem and a few others. "It will be a place that, as a community, we can take care of our aged and infirm," she says, describing Klem as no mere drunk, but a resourceful and inventive former electrician for the Grateful Dead. She also tells me the mine in Terlingua was the third largest in the world during World War I, when ammunition was mercury-fired and prices spiked. Once ammo went electric, the place went bust.

Another topic of conversation: "the 4,000-year-old peyote-induced Huichol pictographs" in Seminole Canyon, 250 miles east of Big Bend. She shows me a picture of a wild mural, full of ornate figures and abstract, alive shapes. "Amazing."

I ask her what she thinks it means.

"They were high as kites. How do you know?"

I tell her I'm in need of a vision. "I've been sleeping on friends' couches and hotel rooms. I'm disorganized as hell. I need to get away—from everything."

"I would go out to the Solitario."

Sounds just about right.

Three hours later, I'm driving toward the Solitario in the interior of Big Bend Ranch State Park, to the west of Terlingua. The unearthly blisterlike geological formation is nearly ten miles across and one of the largest and most symmetrical volcanic domes on the planet.

I've taken off my watch and emptied my pockets, and I'm trying to mentally do the same. Unfortunately, I'm preoccupied by a general sense of disorder—the car is strewn with trash and notebooks and dirty clothes and a watermelon I bought a week before in Luling—and a complete lack of preparation. Do I even have a can opener? A mess kit? I do have two cans of beans, tortillas, peanut butter, two oranges, and, of course, one watermelon.

A grasshopper lands on my windshield and slowly slides backward to the wiper.

I drive an hour and a half down a dirt road, not a pterosaur in the sky, thinking of my recent past, unstuck in time, embarrassments, triumphs. The closer I get to the Solitario, the vast and empty beauty of the West Texas desert wilderness only gets vaster and emptier. A ranger named Marvin checks me in at the Sauceda visitor center and charges me $28 for the entrance fee, two night's camping, and a bundle of firewood.

My campsite is located by itself in the general vicinity of little else, miles from another site, so naturally I miss the turn and continue down a worsening road, then a hill I wonder if my Saturn will be able to make it back up. After finally admitting my mistake and turning around, I test my Saturn's four-wheeling capabilities and wind up sliding down backward, not unlike the grasshopper that landed on my windshield. Frazzled, I have to floor it in reverse to make it up and over the hill.

After locating the site, I take inventory and realize, sadly, I have no mess kit or fuel for my stove. But I do have a can opener. I'm going to need that wood.

The big hill

My trunk is a jumble of luggage, the backseat a veritable pile of rubbish featuring not only that watermelon, but also an empty box of Alamo crackers, a brochure from a goat dairy, and a piece of my car that fell off on my four-wheeling foray. I take time and sort the trash, brochures, dirty clothes, notebooks, and CDs into piles.

The chaos takes shape into order. Psychedelics would not be good for this outing. I need to pull it together, not push it apart.

Next, I unpack my groceries, my water and my
watermelon, my firewood, my sleeping bag and pad
and inflatable pillow. I survey the car's damage. A few
scratches. The tires withstand my kicks.

This spot is everything I hoped for: isolated and
surrounded by an endless sea of cactus and yucca and
undulating earth, the Solitario unfolding just to the east.
I'm glad I have two nights here.

And I'm going to eat that entire watermelon, whether
I like it or not.

I watch the sunset as intently as I can, until the last
trickle of that thermonuclear orange orb drips below
the mountains on the western horizon. Then it's time for
jeans, a hat, and a jacket, as thirteen hours of darkness
begins. I realize just how alone I am out here.

The sunset's residual orange and purple fades to
black and the first stars emerge. Insects chirp. The moon
is nearly full. I get my gloves. A plane passes overhead.

I meticulously prepare the fire pit with plenty of
paper kindling and a pyramid of wood. Then I pace.

Is that Mars? Or is it Jupiter? And who was that
woman with the Obama sticker on her car and the towel
on her head at the ranger station? She said hi. I wonder
where she is now. Then there are the deadlines, the
words to be written, the miles to be driven, the bills to
be paid.

I breathe deep. One day, one night at a time.

The fire starts on the first match. Once the coals
are hot enough—and after I learn watermelon rind is
not flammable—I open a can of baked beans and cook it
over the flames. I watch a piece of ash disintegrate into
nothing. Once the beans are bubbling, I move the can to
the site's picnic table and eat them with three tortillas.

Replaying the memory of my ill-advised excursion
down the hill, I blow up my sleeping pad and lie on it next
to the fire. The night sky keeps adding stars. Coyotes
howl near and far. The moon is bright, a mirror for the
sun that disappeared not long ago.

After one last slab of watermelon, I throw one last allotted log on the fire and "watch the campfire television," as Cynta put it earlier. Someone recently told me a person's brain waves are different under the influence of TV and campfire. I can feel that.

Time to unroll the sleeping bag and blow up my pillow. I sleep a few hours, wake up to a moon nearing the horizon, and fall back asleep to an infinitely detained night sky.

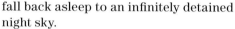

The hopper gorges

Dawn brings more coyote howls, then the chirps of birds, and the buzzes of grasshoppers. It is officially daytime. The sun warms my black sleeping bag from snuggly to uncomfortably warm—I get up. A big, black-and-yellow grasshopper ambles over to the unburned watermelon rinds and sinks his mandibles into one. I cut another piece and follow suit—I still have a long way to go. The grasshopper and I masticate in silence.

I again start a fire with the first match and make some morning coffee. Lacking a mess kit or a pot of any kind, I make my coffee in the clean bean can from the night before.

After taking my time to pack a daypack with water, lunch, two cameras, and an extra layer of clothing—my 35mm camera's lens juts from the top, too bulky to be entirely zipped in—I begin my hike by descending the same hill I barely ascended the night before. I'm flabbergasted that my little Saturn actually conquered the thing.

In the valley of green and gold and gray below, it's a perfect day, warm and breezy, bursting with the savage glory of a truly empty space, devoid of *Homo sapiens*, except one.

Does my rambling make me alone?

There is plenty of life out here. Another black-and-yellow grasshopper sits languidly in the middle of the trail. It looks just like the one who feasted on the rind earlier, and its slowness makes me think it could be the same bloated one. Next up is a grasshopper with a hulking carapace of armor, then a flock of birds hidden in the cacti, then a cactus growing from a rock. A rare patch of mud is ringed with butterflies and dotted with paw prints.

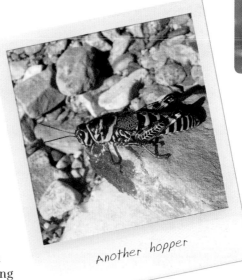

Another hopper

You can be alone in a crowd, or together with just one other. You can anguish over loneliness or cherish it.

The trail drops into a wash with the remnants of the last thunderstorm. A roadrunner dashes across the trail and disappears over a rocky outcropping. In the slender stream of water, a clump of algae stops on a dime. I look closer. It's not algae, it's an amphibian: a spotted khaki toad smaller than my thumbnail. I pick him up for a quick snapshot then return him to water's edge.

"We are all in this alone," as Lily Tomlin so aptly put it, but that's not a bad thing. We all need to be alone from time to time.

Walking up the wash, I realize the toad is not alone.

A very small toad

There are hundreds of these dinky suckers, perfectly camouflaged in the drab gray sand. If they stayed put, I wouldn't even see them, but they can't help but hop out of my path as I head toward a dry gully that advances into the Solitario.

It's slow going, hoisting myself over boulders and across ledges as I work up the trench carved by literally millions of floods over the eons. After a mile or so, it's time for lunch in a shady spot between igneous walls, under an obsidian monolith. I quietly munch on a tortilla full of peanut butter and absentmindedly gaze at the mazes on each of my fingertips.

Something tickles my neck. I grab at it and come away with an infuriated bee. It proceeds to impale my forefinger with his stinger. There is pain but no swelling. I continue up the gully.

A bone of some kind juts from the sand. Another watermelon-loving grasshopper, but this one is dead, dry and desiccated.

In front of me is a rock that slants upward under a thorny tree. I have to crawl to make it under the branches, but one of them manages to catch my camera and fling it into the rocky chasm below. The damage is somewhere between minor and catastrophic.

But you can't dwell on mistakes, lest they become future distractions. I continue worming my way into the colorful heart of the Solitario, rocks towering in the blue sky above, red and pink and white. A walking stick lands on my arm and climbs down my outstretched hand onto a branch of a small tree. Nonwalking sticks tipped with thorns and spines occasionally tear at my flesh as I pass.

At last I scurry up to a ledge where my progress is impeded by ten-foot boulders. Here, I sit in awe, gaping at the view in front of me. This is my place, at least for a brief moment. The last person to sit here is a mystery. I may well be the first.

This is also the place where I turn back and retrace my steps, past the monolith, past the tiny toads, through the

The view from the Solitario

wide canyon, and up the hill my car could only conquer in reverse. I make it back to my camp just in time for sunset. A pair of Texas longhorns mosey by on the road. The big blotchy male stares me down.

"How you doing, cows?" These might well be the first words I've said all day.

And once again, the coyotes howl, the insects chirp, and I repeat the same drill as the night before. Start fire. Check. Can of beans. Check. Burn watermelon rind. Check. Campfire TV. Check. Sleeping bag. Check. Wake up and stare at the stars for a couple of hours. Check.

Soon enough, that big nuclear orb is warming my bag from the eastern horizon. My mind feels back on track, but my body could use a shower. And my feet are still shockingly white.

So after saying good-bye to the longhorns on my way out, I pay a visit to the mildew-stained shower at park headquarters, and drive two hours back to the slightly more populated world of Terlingua. There I drop off a two-gallon water jug I borrowed from Cynta and head north toward an even more densely populated world.

But on my way there, I have to go through a Border Patrol checkpoint. I roll the window down.

"Are you a US citizen?" an agent asks.

"Yes, I am," I reply.

"Are you from around here or just visiting?"

"Just visiting—I went camping in Big Bend Ranch State Park."

"How was it?"

"It was great. I didn't see anyone for thirty-six hours."

"Sometimes we need that."

I nod and drive away, half a watermelon in the passenger seat.

Where to go...

Balmorhea State Park
Four miles west of
Balmorhea on TX Hwy. 17
432-375-2370
www.tpwd.state.tx.us

Million Barrel Museum
400 Museum Blvd.,
Monahans

**Marfa Chamber of
Commerce**
207 N. Highland Ave., Marfa
432-729-4942
www.marfacc.com

Museum of the Big Bend
On the campus of Sul Ross
State University, Alpine
432-837-8730
www.sulross.edu/~museum

Terlingua Ghostown
www.historic-terlingua.com

La Posada Milagro
Terlingua Ghostown
432-371-3044
www.laposadamilagro.com

La Kiva
FM 170, Terlingua
431-371-2250
www.lakiva.net

The Boathouse
Terlingua Ghostown
432-371-2219

**Big Bend Ranch
State Park**
Northeast of Presidio
432-358-4444
www.tpwd.state.tx.us

RAMBLE MANIFESTO

From the second I wake, the pull is strong. My soul once again demands motion. I've slept in the same bed every night for nine weeks or so, about sixty sleeps in all. It's time to go.

At some point in recent memory, I was just as ready for home as I am now ready for the road. Before this homebound stint, I'd been on the road for the better part of two months, driving from the West Texas badlands to the Rockies to Venice Beach, California. Cut to the present: I've only ventured more than fifty miles from home a couple of times in the sixty days since.

All of that stability adds up. I've been sitting too still for too long. The coffee isn't helping quell my nomadic impulses, to be sure; instead it fuels the restlessness building in the pit of my gut. Day after day, the feeling has gotten stronger and stronger and by now I've convinced myself the only cure is the road. Regardless of my diagnostic accuracy, I go through the rituals of preparation. I pack a bag of clothes, a smaller bag of toiletries, a backpack, a camera bag, and assorted other bags of various sizes.

I get up early. I load my car. I fill my travel mug with coffee. I double-check everything. I say good-bye to the dog and leave a key under the mat.

Then I go.

After a passing thought regarding the position of the coffeemaker's power switch, I recline into my new role. Roles, actually: driver, traveler, nomad. A man going on a journey, a stranger coming to town.

That first morning, that's the road trip big bang, where it all begins. What happened before departure is no longer relevant. Home and bills and jobs and everything else in the rearview mirror can wait. There is no better diversion from reality than the road.

Home is yin to the road's yang. The conceptual schism between the two is akin to that of the mind's left and right hemispheres, or that of order and chaos. You can't have one without the other. Home is static, stable, and studied—I know most every corner and get more intimate with the place as the clock ticks ahead. Surprises are few, but comforts are many. But you can get too comfortable. Such is the hazard of home.

The road, conversely, is impossible to know like home. Each bend holds the promise of the new, the unique, the unknown. Habit and routine take a backseat to the buzz of discovery, as mile markers and thoughts of all kinds punctuate the long distances driven.

You can get too precise in your daily routine. You can only gargle your name-brand mouthwash for exactly sixty seconds so many times before you want to kick the day-to-day to the curb. Waking leads to coffee leads to work to lunch to a workout or a daily application of facial cleanser or TV programming or prescription medication. Routine overwhelms everything else; you can actually feel habits cementing into timeworn modes of thought and existence that will be nearly impossible to change. Which brings us back to the relative chaos of the road. The opiate of perpetual motion can salve a soul.

It might sound like I want to take a vacation from myself. It's not entirely untrue. There is also the thought that external motion can provoke internal discovery. Life is a journey, and the road trip is a microcosmic symbol of the mortal trek toward enlightenment. Whatever.

My personal angle stems from the desire for a superlative freedom, for those intangible sensations that start in my gut and oscillate along the very center of my being. It's hard to get such primeval juices flowing from the comfort of a sofa, the gentle refrains of TV ads selling your soul into submission. But that's where these words are spilling out of my pen—a cozy dining table in a living room—as my right leg twitches, the rubber on the tip of my tennis shoe squeaking softly on the hardwood. Sure, home is nice. Home is where the heart is. Home sweet home. There's no place like home.

But there's no place like the road either. The predictability of home ultimately fuels the urge to roam. There's that burning desire to simply move. There's an allure of velocity that only velocity can placate.

There is nothing in life quite like cruising into a classic Western landscape, radio all the way up, windows all the way down, the sunshine and the beauty and the velocity! Velocity is all-important. Without movement, the road ceases to be. Velocity is the road.

The road calls, and I must listen. And why not? It beats sitting around at home all to hell.

The American road is an endless strip of neon-lit blacktop, lined with billboards, cacti, mountains, urban sprawl, toxic waste, and open space, at once desolate and inspiring and lonely and alive.

The road is also a temporary, ephemeral place. It pulses with activity with or without me, as life stories zoom by at eighty miles an hour. Motion is the norm; to move is to exist. The lack of motion is met with puzzlement and suspicion. Stopping is not a legitimate option.

I drive for hours in a meditative state. Then I think, "Well, I wonder what it's like to live here?" At some point, I realized that just about every last spot on the planet was home to somebody. It's the same old shit to somebody.

What exactly the same old shit is depends on geography, but it is everywhere.

Except the road. Those fleeting periods of velocity are some of the purest feelings of freedom available. The road is just the place to get lost. And in my mind, that's a good thing.

Caffeine and long-distance driving are inseparable to me. Without coffee, it's doubtful I'd make it very far, mentally or physically. A cup of joe is the ignition for my imagination and inspiration.

I typically refill my travel mug every time I stop. If I chug sixteen ounces of coffee per tank of gas, there is very little chance I'll snooze. Between the caffeine and the sheer volume of fluid, my mind and bladder work hand in hand to keep me awake.

Another essential: music. Beauty is in the ear of the beholder, but the first rule of the road is that you can never have too much music. On a 5,000-mile journey, you could easily listen to 100 different albums and not repeat once. For those types of trips, a serious library is required. Or a well-stocked iPod.

I don't want to dawdle, but I don't want to rush either. Roadside motels are fine en route, but there better be something better at the end of the line. Greasy spoons provide sustenance, but it's best to have sandwich supplies and a steady stream of hot coffee.

Habit can evolve into a near science. Then I beg for a change, the phone to ring, an e-mail to arrive, anything…

But nothing happens. And it won't, not unless I can will it so. And the confines of routine cannot involve driving halfway across the country, unless you drive a large vehicle for a living. To make it happen, I must go.

But the wise traveler prepares. There are certain necessities. Clothes, and an organizational system for clean clothes, dirty clothes, and those clothes in between. That usually involves a large mothership bag that remains in the trunk, a satellite bag to bring toiletries and a change into motel rooms and friends' places, and a third bag for the stuff that's in need of a wash.

A full array of camping equipment is another must-have, to shave the lodging costs down and give opportunity to park the car and venture into the woods for a day or three.

Then there's the cooler, which sits in the backseat and occasionally hosts soft drinks and sandwich ingredients. Ice is kept to a minimum.

There's a backpack filled with books and notepads and pens and the like in the front seat, along with an assortment of compact discs with jazz, punk, and country songs. There's a laptop and a camera in the back.

Then there are the little things that suit one's tastes, maybe breath mints, drinking water, and marijuana...just don't get caught in the red states.

If you leave at the crack of dawn, it is an incredible feeling to rub your eyes at 9 AM and realize you are nearly 300 miles from home. It would take the pioneers weeks to make it this far. St. Louis to San Francisco was once a harrowing four-month journey. Today it's easy enough to do it in two days.

Indeed, the comfort of the couch and the mind-jelling television and the worn pathways of routine, the guaranteed paychecks and the fifteen-minute breaks, can coalesce into a prison.

APPENDIX: INFO, ETC.

State

Texas Tourism
800-888-8839
www.traveltex.com

Major Convention and Visitors Bureaus and Chambers of Commerce

**Austin Convention
and Visitors Bureau**
800-926-2282
www.austintexas.org

**Dallas Convention
and Visitors Bureau**
800-232-5527
www.visitdallas.com

**Fort Worth Convention
and Visitors Bureau**
800-433-5747
www.fortworth.com

**San Antonio Convention
and Visitors Bureau**
800-447-3372
www.visitsanantonio.com

**Greater Houston Convention
and Visitors Bureau**
800-446-8786
www.visithoustontexas.com

**Corpus Christi Convention
and Visitors Bureau**
800-678-6232
www.corpuschristicvb.com

**El Paso Convention Center
and Visitors Bureau**
800-351-6024
www.elpasocvb.com

**Laredo Convention and
Visitors Bureau**
800-361-3360
www.visitlaredo.com

**Brownsville Convention
and Visitors Bureau**
800-626-2639
www.brownsville.org

**McAllen Convention and
Visitors Bureau**
956-682-2871
www.mcallen.org

**Del Rio Convention and
Visitors Bureau**
800-889-8149
www.drchamber.com

**Fredericksburg Convention
and Visitors Bureau**
888-997-3600
www.fredericksburg-texas.com

**Greater New Braunfels
Chamber of Commerce**
800-572-2626
www.nbcham.org

**Amarillo Convention and
Visitors Council**
800-692-1338
www.visitamarillotx.com

**Lubbock Convention and
Visitors Bureau**
800-692-4035
www.visitlubbock.org

**Midland Convention and
Visitors Bureau**
800-624-6435
www.visitmidlandtexas.com

**Odessa Convention
and Visitors Bureau**
800-780-4678
www.odessacvb.com

Alpine Tourism Initiative
800-561-3712
www.alpinetexas.com

**Marfa Chamber of
Commerce**
800-650-9696
www.marfacc.com

Organizations

Texas Hotel and Lodging
Association
800-856-4328
www.texaslodging.com

Texas Restaurant Association
800-395-2872
www.restaurantville.com

**United States Customs and
Border Protection**
877-227-5511
www.cbp.gov

**Texas Parks and
Wildlife Department**
800-792-1112
www.tpwd.state.tx.us

**Texas State Historical
Association**
940-369-5200
www.tshaonline.org

Transportation

**Texas Department of
Transportation**
800-558-9368
www.txdot.gov

**Austin-Bergstrom
International Airport**
512-530-2242
www.ci.austin.tx.us/austinairport

Dallas/Fort Worth International Airport
972-973-8888
www.dfwairport.com

Dallas Love Field
214-670-6073
www.dallas-lovefield.com

San Antonio International Airport
210-207-3411
www.sanantonio.gov/airport

Houston Airport System
281-233-3000
www.fly2houston.com

El Paso International Airport
915-780-4749
www.elpasointernational
airport.com

Amtrak
800-872-7245
www.amtrak.com

National Parks and Monuments

Big Bend National Park
432-477-2251
www.nps.gov/bibe

Guadalupe Mountains National Park
915-828-3251
www.nps.gov/gumo

Padre Island National Seashore
361-949-8068
www.nps.gov/pais

Amistad National Recreation Area
830-775-7491
www.nps.gov/amis

Big Thicket National Preserve
409-951-6725
www.nps.gov/bith

Lake Meredith National Recreation Area and Alibates Flint Quarries National Monument
806-857-3151
www.nps.gov/lamr
www.nps.gov/alfl

INDEX